Charter Schools

A REFERENCE HANDBOOK

Other Titles in
ABC-CLIO's
CONTEMPORARY EDUCATION ISSUES
Series

FORTHCOMING

African American Education, Cynthia Jackson
Bilingual Education, Rosa Castro Feinberg
Special Education, Arlene Sacks
Student Rights, Patricia H. Hinchey

CONTEMPORARY EDUCATION ISSUES

Charter Schools

A REFERENCE HANDBOOK

Danny Weil

Santa Barbara, California • Denver, Colorado • Oxford, England

© 2000 by Danny Weil

Library of Congress Cataloging-in-Publication Data

Weil, Danny K., 1953–
    Charter schools : a reference handbook / Danny Weil.
        p. cm. — (Contemporary education issues)
Includes bibliographical references and index.
    ISBN 1-57607-245-2
    1. Charter schools—United States. I. Title. II. Series.
    LB2806.36.W45 2000
    371.01'0973—dc21

                                                    00-011351

This book is also available on the World Wide Web as an e-book. Visit www.abc-clio.com for details.

06 05 04 03 02 01 00   10 9 8 7 6 5 4 3 2 1

ABC-CLIO, Inc.
130 Cremona Drive, P.O. Box 1911
Santa Barbara, California 93116-1911

This book is printed on acid-free paper ∞.
Manufactured in the United States of America

*This book is dedicated to
Lenny Sandroff—teacher, learner,
parent, grandparent, and my friend—whom I
loved very, very much
(September 23, 1946–June 19, 2000)*

Contents

vii

☙ Preface

This book seeks to examine and discuss the charter school movement and the particular controversies that surround public choice and charter schools as an educational reform effort. The charter school movement is compared and contrasted with other educational innovations that have been historically important for education in the United States, such as vouchers, magnet schools, school choice, privatization, alternative schools, on-site management, and changes in standards and assessment. In this book, I look at what has motivated the development of the charter school reform movement—from the frustration of parents, teachers, and students to the hopes and aspirations of community members and educational policymakers—and attempt to delineate the historical development of the movement by providing a historical chronology.

I also examine the organization and development of specific charter schools in several states and briefly look at the curriculum of various charter schools in others. I explore the laws that govern charter schools as well as the history and politics that surround the charter school movement and discuss the steps in developing a charter school and how both legislation and politics define and maintain the charter school effort as an educational controversy in today's society.

Finally, the book includes a directory of organizations, associations, and government agencies associated with the charter school movement as well as a bibliography of print and nonprint resources.

Chapter One

➳ Introduction

THE EMERGENCE OF CHARTER SCHOOLS

Shortly after the start of the 1990s, the American public witnessed one of the most significant and controversial developments in public education: the emergence of the charter school movement. Until 1991, there was no such thing as a charter school (a public school under contract) in the United States. The idea, in its embryonic state, had not been embraced by any state in the union, and, in fact, no state had passed charter school legislation. Yet by late 1998, the development of numerous charter schools had been legitimized and was supported by charter school legislation in thirty-four states and the District of Columbia.

By 1998, more than 1,100 charter schools had emerged and were educating more than a quarter of a million students. The states involved allowed the public to begin the charter school experiment, freeing many charter schools from state laws and school district policies and regulations. The idea was relatively simple—although complex in its controversial implications—for charter school proponents claimed they were looking to stimulate new and innovative educational opportunities and to provide parents and communities with alternatives to traditional public schooling through "choice." Charter school advocates argued that charter school legislation and the development of local charter schools would stimulate competition, raise educational standards throughout public schools, allow for local governance, and stimulate reform and improvement throughout the entire educational system. Many educational constituencies within communities, ranging from parents to teachers, argued that charter schools should be community-based schools and hold the promise of breaking up large, factory-style schools and burdensome and often nonfriendly educational bureaucracies and administrations.

Politicians, from governors to state legislators, looked to charter schools as an antidote to what they saw as the failure of public schools, lack of educational innovation, barriers to parent and student involvement, and lackluster educational accountability. Proponents of charter schools argued that charter schools would serve as a magical cure in an era of public school mediocrity and top-heavy educational bureaucra-

1

cies, and the idea became a popular and hotly debated one among a diverse community of educational workers, parents, local neighborhoods, and students.

Part of the widespread appeal of charter schools lies in the perception, right or wrong, that the public schools are not serving the needs of their students, the teachers that labor within them, the parents of the students that attend them, or the community at large that supports them. Proponents of charter schools argue that politics, coupled with public schools that are mired in burdensome bureaucracy and historically administratively top-heavy, simply will not and cannot reform the school systems.

Conservative politicians and their adherents admire the charter idea because, they insist, charter schools provide a way to avoid oppressive government regulations and can operate under the auspices of competition and choice—and allegedly produce educational results superior to those produced by the current public school systems. Progressive politicians promote charter schools as a way to use freedom from regulation to create innovative centers of learning that are community based and can serve as a source for revitalized community participation in local schools. These politicians look to the charter idea as an opportunity born from the historical struggle to personalize learning and make the educational curriculum relevant to students. They also look at charter schools as an environment that has low teacher-to-student ratios and in which there are many personal opportunities for contact between students and teachers—an environment in which experimentation with a wide range of instructional techniques, including individualized and cooperative approaches to learning, can be undertaken with the aim of upgrading the general quality of instruction.

Many nonwhite constituencies, such as African American parents and students, support the charter school concept precisely because, as many of them claim, traditional public schools have failed those students. These people argue that allowing them to choose what kind of school their children will attend will ensure that their children will be given an equal opportunity to learn.

As shall be seen, many proponents of charter schools argue that such schools create options that cannot be found in the current public school approaches, and they also maintain that charter schools provide neighborhoods with the chance to govern their own community-based schools through decentralization and site-based management principles. These factors, they argue, provide elements of control, ownership, and democracy that are not found in the unbalanced, bureaucratic, and system-wide public school districts. They reason that a smaller class size, the ability to pay individual attention to students, and relevant, personalized learning are just some of the benefits of charter schools.

Because charter schools are governed by private boards, usually nonprofit in nature though increasingly managed for profit, advocates argue that such schools are a way to assert community ownership of and control over schools and allow parents and educators to participate in, indeed compose, the agenda and curriculum development of schooling. Many educational policymakers of all political persuasions also argue that charter schools provide a way to implement reforms without mandating them hierarchically within politically mired public school districts. The policymakers claim such school districts often fail to implement necessary reforms and changes owing to the highly charged and diverse educational debates that run rampant among the various constituencies that compose them.

Many progressive educators who support charter schools also argue that they are a way to prevent the privatization of schooling sought through conservative calls for vouchers and so-called school choice. In an economic and social environment in which deregulated markets and privatization of social institutions are looked at as solutions to social problems, these educators look to the charter school idea as a stopgap to prevent total market domination of education. Veteran community activists have begun to embrace charter schools, as have other community activists and talented educators. They insist that public schools can work, and work well, if they are constructed correctly and arranged for the interest of the communities and the students. These progressive educators promote charter schools as a public reform measure in the interest of collaborative experimentation and a creative implementation of new ideas—as a way to save public education through change.

WHO SELECTS CHARTER SCHOOLS?

On average, the charter schools in most states seem to serve the same types of students as are found in the regular public school systems. Studies have found that

- Most charter schools are small. The median enrollment in 1996–1997 was 150 students; it was 500 in other public schools in states with charter schools.
- More than 60 percent of charter schools enrolled fewer than 200 students, and only 16 percent of regular public schools had fewer than 200 students.

- Three in five, or 60 percent, of the charter schools are brand new institutions, 25 percent of them were converted from existing public schools, and 13 percent of them were converted from existing private schools.
- In 1996–1997, about 42 percent of the students in charter schools were nonwhite and about 40 percent were nonwhite in the existing public schools of sixteen charter states. Some 36 percent of charter students were eligible for a free or reduced-price lunch compared to about 40 percent in regular public schools (Hassel 1999, 1).
- Urban areas are particularly fertile grounds for the development of charter schools because there is a great deal of disenchantment with local urban public schools. A study done in 1996, which included 225 charter schools in seven states, found that the minority group members in urban areas composed a large proportion of the student body—63 percent (Schwartz 1996, 4).

DOES EVERYONE SUPPORT CHARTER SCHOOLS?

Not all people are sold on the idea of charter schools. Many progressive educational policy analysts criticize charter schools for their potential to further stratify schools along racial, socioeconomic, and other ethnic- and class-based lines. They feel that charter schools may be the first step toward the privatization of education and are concerned that charter schools will skim or "cream off" predominantly white, privileged students from public schools and thus contribute to the segregation of schools in the United States (Schwartz 1996, 4). They also argue that the propensity for charter schools to cream off students would result in ethnically concentrated schools of choice and are concerned about the ability of charter schools to provide services for all students, such as students with disabilities and special educational needs. And they are worried that exclusionary and selective admission policies and practices might contribute to racial imbalances among schools and promote the return of the concept of "separate but equal" along racial lines in the United States (Cobb and Glass, 1999). They maintain that this situation can be accomplished institutionally through measures such as charter school legislation just as well as through an overt return to racial segregation.

For example, one institutional concern that has been disturbingly absent from charter school reform discussions is the issue of transportation for inner city students who often have to travel long distances to attend these schools. On the issue of transportation, a

Carnegie Foundation report points out that for all schools the median distance between families and their closest school is two miles, the median distance to the next closest school is four and a half miles, and for one in four families, the next closest school is between ten and eighty miles away (Carnegie Foundation 1992).

Transportation is a large issue for charter schools for two reasons: one, the increase in the amount families must pay to send their children to charter schools and, two, the amount of time that children are forced to spend in transit to and from these schools. Districts that have absorbed the cost of transportation have found that subsidizing transportation for charter schools can cost thousands of dollars. Many educators leery of charter schools claim that transportation is one of those institutional issues that must be watched if charter schools are not to become an unassuming partner in a further stratification of society along racial and class lines.

Many crucial questions need to be asked regarding charter schools. At this point in time, all concerned constituents interested in the issue—proponents, opponents, and those who just do not know—agree there is too little evidence about the efficacy of charter schools and their impact on educational reform. Some of the questions that must be asked might include, Do charter schools have a responsibility to parents and students to offer a diverse community of learners? Will charter schools lead to a further desegregation of U.S. schools and the privatization of education? Is choice really good? Will competition really increase educational performance? Will charter schools truly provide choice to all constituencies regardless of class background, disability, or ethnicity? Will transportation to and from these schools be subsidized by districts or paid for by the students and their parents? Does choice really help bring about reform in public education? Will charters put pressure on the entire public school system to engage in self-corrective practices and policies? Are charter schools really community-based schools and are they really accountable to their communities? Should we allow public schools to be run as educational maintenance organizations by for-profit companies? Do charter schools have a civic obligation to achieve the ethnic representation of the community, given that they are schools of choice with no local attendance boundaries to confine their ethnic compositions? In what ways should the state intervene in cases of de facto segregation or inequity? What should the admission policies look like? These, and no doubt many more, are just a few of the important questions that must be addressed as we assess the impact and implications of charter schools as an educational reform movement.

Whether supported as an innovative idea or rejected as a debilitating fancy, it is certain that the growth of charter schools can claim to be one of the most interesting and controversial experiments in education for many decades. In many ways, the growth of the charter school movement parallels a movement away from traditional, modern answers to educational problems and controversies. The movement is really part of a postmodern, decentralized attempt to wrestle with educational controversy—a shift from centralized systems of control and organization to a more decentralized, devolutionary environment.

The success or failure of the charter school movement is subject to important debate and will have unimaginable implications for the way we as a nation think about and organize schooling. Improvement in student achievement; local control; issues of equity, race, gender, and class; and the impact of charter schools on public school systems—all of these issues and more still remain to be explored and analyzed. It may take years to actually trace, analyze, and understand the impact of charter schools. However, with charter laws in existence in more than thirty states and three or more years of implementation in more than fifteen states, research is becoming available, and people interested in education, from teachers to students and from parents to politicians, are looking at this controversial educational movement with watchful eyes.

DEFINING A CHARTER SCHOOL

Charter schools are public schools under contract—called a charter. These contracts, or charters, are granted from a public agency to a group of parents, teachers, school administrators, nonprofit agencies, organizations, or businesses that wish to create an alternative to existing public schools in order to provide choice within the public school system. Charter schools receive public money and cannot legally discriminate or exclude students. They are also publicly accountable; thus, they are not private schools (Council of Urban Boards 1997). This important distinction is often missed, and it is also important to realize that charter schools are not alternative schools. Rather, they are legal entities that exist under a public contract, and anyone who wishes to start a charter school must negotiate the contract, or charter, with the local school district or state body that is empowered to approve the charter. Charter schools are held to the educational accountability standards that have been adopted in their state and district.

Nearly all charter schools are either "conversions" (preexisting public schools or, less commonly, private schools transformed into charter schools) or start-ups (new schools that would not otherwise exist). According to a study of charter schools by the University of Minnesota for the U.S. Department of Education, 56.4 percent of the charter schools operating in 1995–1996 were new, 32.5 percent were once regular public schools, and 11.1 percent had been private schools (Hudson Institute 1997, pt. 6, 2).

Typically, contracts, or charters, are granted for a three- to five-year period. The charter school receives public funding at or around the per-pupil level of other public schools in the district in which it operates. In the charter itself, the applicants must delineate and explain how the school will operate, what courses and curriculum will be offered, what outcomes will be achieved by students, and how state standards and assessment will measure these outcomes. The charter school must eventually marshal evidence, as a form of accountability, that students in the school have gained the knowledge and skills indicated in the charter. All charter schools operate within strict state guidelines, which vary from state to state.

DIFFERENCES BETWEEN CHARTER SCHOOLS AND OTHER EDUCATIONAL REFORMS

It is important to distinguish between charter schools and other educational reform movements, with which they are often confused.

Vouchers

Although both charter schools and the voucher proposal demand choice and argue that competition is the key to increased public school performance and accountability, the charter school concept is significantly different from the voucher movement. For example, the charter school reform concept provides parents with a *public* choice as to which school they wish their children to attend—not a *private* choice. Families who are given private vouchers for a specific amount of public money are thus given a *private* choice. They can use the money to pay tuition at their choice of school—be it public, parochial, or private. Although numerous voucher proposals have been put forward, and many of them have been implemented in one or more states (Friedman 1993), they differ dramatically from the charter school concept in four distinct ways (Nathan 1996).

First, charter schools cannot be sectarian. Vouchers allow students to attend either a public or a private parochial school, but public funds, which pay for charter schools, cannot be used for sectarian or private school education. Second, in most states, charter school legislation does not allow schools to pick and choose among applicants on the basis of previous achievement or behavior. This restriction differs dramatically from the voucher concept as voucher plans state that schools may choose the students who will attend the schools in any way the schools wish. This difference in admission policy has been one of the key reasons why charter schools have been accepted and embraced as an idea for educational reform by many public school defenders. However, how this restriction translates into practice—as mentioned earlier regarding race, equity, "skimming," "creaming," and other selective admission policies—is the subject of debate.

Third, voucher proposals permit private and parochial schools to charge as much tuition as they wish, above and beyond the public money given to parents for their children, and parents must then pay the difference with their own money. Charter schools, on the other hand, cannot charge any tuition beyond the state allocation they receive.

The final difference between vouchers and charter schools is the explicit responsibility for documenting student achievement. To keep and renew their charters, charter schools are held publicly accountable to state educational standards and must demonstrate that their students are improving their skills and expanding their knowledge base. Voucher schools, on the other hand, have no public accountability requirements and no responsibility to publicly document or assure student achievement other than that proposed by the school itself.

Magnet Schools

Magnet schools are public schools with specialized curricula designed to attract particular students from within a given school district. They are often found in urban districts as part of a desegregation or student-at-risk program. Their stated intent is to bring students together from distinct and diverse racial and cultural backgrounds to share a common educational experience. Unlike other public schools, many magnet schools have admission tests and requirements (Steel and Levine 1994). Also, the amount of money spent on a magnet school within a local school district can be far more than that spent on other schools in the same district. Surveys have found that magnet schools in Chicago, Philadelphia, Boston, and New York received extra resources beyond those given to other local public schools in the same state (Hughes 1988). Magnet schools are often given greater funding because they are often perceived as being experimental and innovative. Their intention is not to create communities of learning that will compete with other public schools; they are part and parcel of the public school process and offer innovation within the system.

By contrast, a key distinction in the charter school strategy is that charter schools do not receive more than the state per-pupil average spent on education. This distinction becomes, for charter school advocates, a case of financial equity. Many charter school proponents argue that if charter schools are really to meet the challenges of educational innovation and thus show the value of public school choice, they should do so with the same per-pupil financial resources the other public schools receive. In other words, the public choice competition should occur on a level playing field with regard to funding. However, the costs of beginning and starting a charter school can be high, and these costs are often met through obtaining private grants and corporate sponsorship.

Also, magnet schools are under no requirement to demonstrate that the skills and knowledge of their students have improved whereas charter schools are held publicly accountable for student achievement and student improvement through their contractual relationship with the public. Finally, magnet schools are started exclusively by school districts while charters can be sponsored, depending on the state, by a host of patrons.

Privatization of Schools

The movement toward market-driven solutions to perceived public educational problems has fostered the reemergence of a private voucher system that was first advocated about 1955. Market-driven solutions to educational issues promise that unregulated free choice between private and public schools will serve as a panacea for what ails education in the United States. Market-reform advocates argue that allowing parents to choose between a private and a public school will increase competition among the schools and benefit educational reforms systemwide. They advocate giving parents public vouchers so the parents could choose any school—sectarian or nonsectarian, private or public.

Charter schools are a form of public choice only, which means that charter schools remain public schools and are thus held to public accountability as well as being accountable to state and federal laws regarding equal protection and separation of church and state. Public choice differs from private choice when parents are able to choose among public schools, some of which are charter schools. The parents are not given public money that they might use to send their children to private schools.

The privatization of education as an answer to what ails U.S. schools has been hotly debated within the educational and political system for some time now. And although the debate has focused primarily on providing public vouchers to send children to private schools, the hiring of private companies to run public schools is also closely associated with privatization, and, as we will see, private companies are increasingly being used to run charter schools. This social and economic arrangement allows for the payment of public moneys to these private companies because they are contracted to run public schools. These commercial educational companies appeal to local school districts to give them contracts to run and operate public charter schools within the designs, concepts, and curricula developed by the private companies. The companies then hire the teachers who carry out the formulated educational curriculum and plans. This practice seems in theory to be precisely the opposite of the goals of charter schools because charter schools claim to be based on a philosophy that is the opposite of that of privately run public schools. Whether this difference actually exists in every case is another question.

The advocates of charter schools claim that one of the central objectives of charter schools is to empower classroom teachers, administrators, and parents by giving them the opportunity to create the schools that they feel will help the students. Whereas corporate privatization seeks to remove control from teachers and parents, charter schools seek to place control of the schools directly in the hands of the educational stakeholders. At least, that is the stated claim of many proponents (Kolderie 1993, 1).

Also, the role of unions and collective bargaining is reevaluated and jeopardized in the privatized corporate model for education. With charter schools, collective bargaining can remain intact, and schools or school districts, depending on the state charter legislation, must continue to negotiate with teachers regarding their salaries and working conditions if the teachers so choose. Because educational companies that run public charter schools often can hire and fire the teachers they want at will, the role of unions and collective bargaining can become a serious issue for educational workers, parents, and students.

School On-Site Management

On-site school management, or what is often called shared decision making, differs from the charter concept in one important manner—accountability and responsibility for student performance and achievement. Although charter schools are required to document and demonstrate improvement in the achievement and performance of students, there is no accountability requirement with regard to the school site-management concept.

The site-management idea derives from the belief that if schools are run by the faculty, administrators, and parents, in a partnership so to speak, the schools will be more effective because educational decisions will be made by the educational stakeholders. Delegating authority to on-site councils, site-management advocates claim, will increase student achievement and have a direct and positive impact on how schools are run and operated. Critical decisions about budget, personnel, curriculum, and instruction can be made by on-site management councils or similar governing bodies made up of diverse interested parties, and this fact, advocates maintain, puts the politics of education and educational decisions directly where they belong—in the hands of parents, teachers, administrators, and students.

Even though many charter school advocates probably would agree with decentralizing control and power to the school site, they argue that along with the power to make decisions must come the power to be held accountable to some set of educational standards. Furthermore, they argue, on-site management, by itself, has done little to achieve effectiveness and higher educational performance (Summers and Johnson 1994).

For most charter schools, on-site management is relevant in how these schools organize their decision making and problem solving regarding educational issues. On-site management within charter schools is seen more as a way of governance than as an end in itself.

The Debate over Educational Standards and Assessment

Given the debate that is currently raging regarding the type of standards and assessments that should be used in public schools, the question arises as to the difference between the concept of charter schools and the standards and accountability debate itself. If charters are held to the same standards as traditional public schools, then where is the innovation?

The debate over standards and educational accountability varies depending on whom one talks to on the political spectrum. Charter schools attempt to influence this debate by providing educational choices for parents and students in terms of how their children will meet the standards. Advocates argue that such choices will create a climate of competition among public schools so that all public schools will feel the need to increase their students' performance and knowledge. By putting pressure on the traditional public schools to raise their expectations of students and test scores through competition, many charter school advocates argue that the charter movement is essential in improving the country's educational performance. The assumption is that students do better on tests when they are driven by competitive schools to do so.

However, instead of creating their own standards for accountability, charter schools are held to the educational standards adopted by a particular state and local district (Council of Urban Boards 1997). Thus, they may participate in the state, district, or federal debate regarding standards and assessment, but they cannot create their own assessment outside of the state or district purview.

What many charter schools do instead is to adopt unique and innovative ways of measuring student progress other than the traditional standardized tests—though those are used as well. For example, in a May 1999 study, the U.S. Department of Education assembled a cross-state comparison of the estimated percentage of schools using various types of assessment instruments. The study indicated that in an attempt to meet state standards and assess and evaluate student performance:

- Most charter schools reported that they used standardized assessments of student achievement 86 percent of the time, and 75 percent of the charter schools used tests as part of the state's assessment program.
- Most charter schools reported using student demonstration of knowledge as a way of measuring the school's achievement. Seventy-nine percent used student portfolios and 70 percent used performance assessments to measure student progress.

The study also found that assessment methods were generally consistent for both newly created and preexisting public schools. It was found that preexisting private schools were slightly less likely to use performance assessments, student portfolios, parent surveys, and behavioral indicators to evaluate student performance. On the other hand, preexisting public schools were slightly more likely to use student surveys and behavioral indicators (U.S. Department of Education 1999). Thus, charter schools provide unique and varied opportunities for children to meet state educational standards and to measure their knowledge and performance.

WHY CHARTER SCHOOLS?

There are many reasons why the charter school movement has become so popular. The idea of allowing parents and teachers to create the types of schools they feel will work for them and their communities is just common sense. When that fact is coupled with the myriad of competing philosophies as to what education should be accomplishing, the content of curricula, and what students need to know, charter schools seem like a good idea. Also, many, if not most, people believe that public schools should and could do a better job of helping our nation's young increase their knowledge acquisition and develop critical thinking skills. And while the debate rages over the efficacy of the job public schools are doing, the impetus for the charter school movement, in large part, rests on the assumption that the public schools are not doing enough.

A Nation at Risk, a highly controversial report published in 1983 by the U.S. Department of Education, was highly critical of student achievement in the country's public schools, and in addition to this popular and media-sensationalized report, many educational stakeholders, from parents to teachers, from administrators to students, have historically been concerned that the public school system is not serving the needs of low-income families, varied racial constituencies, and the newly arriving immigrant populations that have increased dramatically since the 1980s. We will look at the incentives and controversies that surround the political realities of the charter movement in a subsequent chapter, but to answer the question, Why charter schools? it is important to examine the philosophical tenets of the movement.

EDUCATIONAL CHOICE

As noted earlier, the impetus for the charter school movement can be found in the idea of "educational choice." The concept is quite simple. The central argument of advocates of choice is that competition provides the best or most efficient way to change the way public schools function. Arguing that removing regulation and dismantling educational bureaucracies will produce better schools, charter school proponents look to such schools to be both beacons for a new alternative to public schools and a force to move the public schools toward greater levels of excellence. The Hudson Institute states the case for charters succinctly.

> The charter concept is simple but powerful: Sound school choices can be provided to families under the umbrella of public education without micro-management by government bureaucracies. Independent schools that are open to all, paid for with tax dollars, accountable to public authorities for student learning and other results, and subject to

basic health, safety, and nondiscrimination requirements, are legitimate public schools even if they are governed or managed by a committee of parents, a team of teachers, the local Boys and Girls Club, or a profit seeking firm. (Hudson Institute 1997, pt. 6, 2)

From the point of view of many liberals and conservatives, charter schools are based on the concept that competition, and only competition, will drive reform and educational change. Veteran charter proponent and pioneer in the movement, Ted Kolderie, has written: "The intent of charter schools is not simply to produce a few new and hopefully better schools. It is to create dynamics that will cause the mainline system to change so as to improve education for all students" (Kolderie 1993, 1). Joe Nathan, another leading reformer in the charter school movement nationwide adds: "The goal of the charter movement is not just to establish innovative schools, but also to help improve the public education system. Charter schools provide families with choices and give skilled, entrepreneurial educators an opportunity, with accountability, to create more effective public schools. They also allow fair competition for public school districts" (Nathan 1996, xxviii).

The primary dynamic, then, is to put competitive pressure on conventional schools—or so it is stated. Many charter school advocates argue that school districts without charter school programs find it easier to ignore the demand for responsive schools that are continually improving and changing.

However, the people who are wary of the charter idea would argue that upon closer scrutiny, it seems that the competition envisioned by charter school advocates as a result of charter school choice is designed to fiscally punish the conventional public schools by imposing costs on the school districts. After all, they argue, when students choose to attend a charter school, that fact removes money from conventional districts as the fiscal system is so designed that the public funding follows the students. As a result, it is likely that school districts will either alter their practices, adopt new ideas and innovations, or face financial difficulties (Hassel 1999, 6).

And just who are the charter school advocates? According to Tom Watkins, director of the Detroit Center for Charter Schools, charter school advocates fall into one of three categories:

1. Zealots, who believe that private is always better than public, market systems are always superior to public systems, unions always cause problems, and students at private and religious schools outperform their public counterparts

2. Entrepreneurs, who hope to make money running schools or school programs
3. Reformers—students, parents, teachers—who want to expand public school options and improve systems of education. (Watkins 1999, 40)

From the point of view of parents and students, the main political attraction of the charter school movement lies in the fact that it gives people of various social, political, cultural, and philosophical backgrounds who are disconnected from the educational system in one way or another an alternative to the regular public schools—i.e., a choice. This demand for "choice" among educational stakeholders led to more than 1,000 charter schools nationwide in just eight years (Wells et al. 1999, 3).

Yet not everybody agrees that competition as a result of choice is the prescription for what plagues public schools. Critics of the idea not only claim that charter schools have the propensity to cream off the best and the most motivated students but argue that charter schools leave regular public schools unable to compete. They maintain that the public schools will suffer from race and class segregation and that charter schools will find ways to deny students with special needs in an attempt to stave off high costs. These people also contend that those schools not chartered will suffer from shoddy educational practices and that charter schools will serve only a handful of students while siphoning off resources that could be devoted to improving the public schools. And, claim critics, school reform that is separated and disconnected from the larger context of financial inequality and power relations in society, that is, the institutional organization of power, control, and authority, cannot hope to work.

According to that reasoning, because of the uneven distribution of material resources across communities, charter school reform essentially serves to fragment or atomize public education into smaller entities—schools as opposed to districts. Also, such reasoning maintains that the isolation and separation of poor communities from each other and from rich communities is actually exacerbated by charter schools (Wells et al. 1999, 19). By segregating and separating the wealthy from the nonwealthy, it is difficult, critics claim, for members of poor, isolated communities to build coalitions based on mutual interests with people who have both the political and the economic means to invest in public services such as schools (Massey and Denton 1993).

In a work entitled *School Choice* (1992), for example, the Carnegie Foundation has argued that advocates for choice have overwhelmingly concentrated their focus on its alleged benefits to individuals and have paid little, if any, attention to how education serves communal and civic purposes. The book states: "Adopting a language of the marketplace, education is portrayed as a solitary act of consumerism. Under systems of choice, advocates say, one can shop around for a school, much as one shops for a VCR, or a new car. The purpose of the enterprise, we are told, is to satisfy 'the customer'" (Carnegie Foundation 1992, 86). The report goes on to argue for the importance of a neighborhood school and is less interested in the ability of students to move freely from one school to another than in the freedom for schools to make their own decisions without webs of regulation.

The charter school experiment promises to be an educational eye-opener for some time to come. And with more and more states legislating charter schools, coupled with federal support for the idea, the explosion in the development of these schools has only just begun.

WHY EDUCATIONAL STAKEHOLDERS CHOOSE CHARTER SCHOOLS

In the 1980s, the development of school choice was believed to be a conservative educational reform recommendation. At that time, opinion polls consistently showed majority support for school choice. In 1986, for instance, a Gallup poll showed that 54 percent of nonwhites supported publicly funded private school choice (Brighouse 1999, 22). As we enter the new millennium, choice has received a boost from the conviction held by individuals of all political persuasions that public education is mired in bureaucracy, particularly in the large cities, and from the hope that allowing families to choose their children's schools might be one way to undermine this educational stranglehold.

Parental Frustration

One of the biggest impetuses for the charter school movement is the frustration experienced by parents of students of all ethnic groups, cultures, and socioeconomic classes regarding the state of the country's current public schools. Although they have very different political reasons and educational priorities, they all desire the same thing: the best possible education for their children. What "the best possible education" means, however, varies.

The concern for high-quality education has united some forces that would otherwise not normally coalesce. For example, the Sequoia

School in Mesa, Arizona, demonstrates the type of flexibility that the charter concept offers parents. At that school, two different educational programs coexist. On the one hand, there is a highly structured back-to-basics curriculum, and on the other, a multi-age, team-taught "progressive" curriculum is offered. Both are being offered at the same school to different students (Hudson Institute 1997, pt. 6, 4). When the Hudson Institute, a Washington, D.C., think tank, studied charter school issues, it found that when parents were asked why they chose charter schools, the top answers were small class size, 53 percent; higher standards, 45.9 percent; educational philosophy, 44 percent; greater opportunities for parental involvement, 43 percent; and better teachers, 41.9 percent (Hudson Institute 1997, pt. 1, 1).

Yet just because many parents have become charter school advocates does not mean that they seek to dismantle public schools; in fact, the contrary can be claimed. By looking to control the public schools through charters, many parents believe they are defending public schools, albeit in a different form. One of the findings that appears to support this contention is a recent opinion poll regarding choice. Those that answered "yes" on the choice question also answered "yes" when asked whether private schools receiving public funds should be regulated by the state like public schools (Hudson Institute 1997, pt. 1, 25).

It is significant to note some of the frustrations that parents have expressed because of the current state of the public schools in order to understand the rapid development of charter schools. In 1988, the Education Commission of the United States released a report indicating what reform efforts might improve the scholastic performance of students in inner city high schools. Among many things, the report found that what was needed was to "establish purposive partnerships in the outside community (with parents, community organizations, private-sector business, colleges and universities, and social service deliverers) as a way to expand resources available to the school, to build a broader constituency for public education, to empower parents and community, and to create access to opportunities (jobs, postsecondary schooling) beyond the schools" (Education Commission of the States 1983, 9).

Instead, parents do not feel they are truly considered a part of the educational process in many public schools, and many of them feel they are left out of the decision-making process that defines education for their children. Parents perceive of themselves as outsiders who are not communicated with but are instead communicated to.

In *The Power of Their Ideas: Lessons for America from a Small School in Harlem* (1995), author and educational activist Deborah Meier argues for school choice and educational innovation. She talks about the frustration of parents because of the enormity and size of urban public schools and the depersonalized learning that too often takes place within their walls. She speaks to parents who express frustration at the lack of respect they receive from the administrators and school personnel of large urban schools, and she narrates the parents' frustration at what they envision as large, factory-style bureaucratic machines that seek to control, rather than give ownership to, parents, teachers, and students. She also discusses the parents' frustration with the type of instruction their children are receiving, the curricula they are subjected to, and the knowledge they are attaining.

The lack of what many parents see as "humanity" in large city schools has certainly been one of the catalysts that has promoted the charter school movement. Parents have sung the praises of charter schools because, they argue, they are able to make democratic and collaborative decisions in small, personal school sites. Knowing the students' names, understanding their needs, and personalizing their learning are matters that parents believe cannot be done in large, centralized schools where the parents perceive, rightly or wrongly, that they have no control or participation in the decision-making process. Educational communities of manageable size that are governed by people who have a stake in the public schools, parents argue, is something that can be accomplished in the smaller charter schools.

A 1997 study of parental involvement in charter schools seems to support the fact that parents who send their children to such schools are much more involved in how the school operates. The findings of the study conducted by an independent researcher and presented at the annual meeting of the American Educational Research Association examined parental participation in one urban and one suburban charter school in the northwestern part of the United States. The study focused on data gathered from interviews with ten parents (six urban and four suburban), a questionnaire filled out by eighteen parents (eight urban and ten suburban), and journals kept by two parents (both urban). The parents cited curriculum, technology, and character education as the reasons for sending their children to charter schools (Anderson 1997). The study also found that in the charter schools studied, especially the urban schools, staff and teachers were encouraged to get parents involved at all levels, which included communicating with them by e-mail, weekly newsletters, and a promise that every phone call would be returned within twenty-four hours (Anderson 1997, 4). The mother of two boys who both attended a charter school commented on one of her sons:

When he was first in the charter, I thought "something new again." But then I saw him flourish, and the teachers took such an interest in him. And in me. They called me, and we worked together. The charter has given me something to connect to. Through it I became interested in the school and really, that was part of why I was willing to serve on the governance council at our high school. I feel it is my school, now, too. (Fine 1994a, 13)

Parental frustration at a lack of relationship with teachers seems to be a universal complaint among parents interviewed. The above study illustrated that having scheduled open communication with teachers and the opportunity to express ideas about the curriculum and philosophy of the schools made parents feel treated as partners in their children's education.

Parents as partners in the classroom is hardly a novel concept, yet many parents assert, with respect to large, urban schools, that they are treated more like den mothers than partners in the classroom. Engaging families in the education of their children and treating them as equals in the classroom, many parents contend, goes a long way in building trust and community commitment and has been found to create long-term and far-reaching results (Scherer 1998).

But parental frustration with large public schools does not end with simply a call for community-based schools that are intimate and small. Another motive for parental support for the charter school idea is dismay about what parents see as crime, gangs, and school violence in the large urban schools; thus, they seek refuge in small, charter schools. Urban charter schools in low-income communities are seen by parents and educators as safe havens from the other nearby public schools, which they often perceive to be dangerous.

Frustration is also expressed at the type of instruction that is found in many large urban schools. Parents around the country have expressed frustration with the kind of learning that is taking place in the schools; the type of instruction and strategies that are employed, from worksheets to fill in the blanks; and the lack of motivation among many of the teachers in these schools.

Many nonwhite parents also argue that instructional strategies employed in many public schools fail to include the contributions of diverse cultural and racial groups in the materials and discriminate on the basis of socioeconomic class. For instance, members of a working-class African American community may want to turn their local public school into a charter school to ensure that their children are exposed to a back-to-the-basics curriculum via the use of technology (Wells et al. 1999, 9).

Parents have also been instrumental in promoting and creating urban, ethnocentric, and grassroots charter schools. Wishing to create a "safe space" or a "home place" for students of a particular racial or ethnic group who live in the surrounding community, parents, educators, and community members in many localities have set up Afro-centric, Chicano-centric, or Native American–centric curricula. These charter schools are born of the frustration of parents in marginalized communities who often feel that the educational system has failed to take their knowledge, their history, and their experiences seriously (Collins 1991).

Grassroots charters, advocates argue, allow for parental involvement in the process of organizing and founding the charter school and therefore can help low-income parents and community members of color create and sustain new social networks that can be used for political organizing and gaining a political voice within the larger society. The argument advanced is that by chartering schools within low-income neighborhoods and among people of color, the process will afford the promise of forging connections between disempowered parents and the education system by enhancing parental participation in the education of the children.

A teacher at one urban grassroots charter school noted that she saw improvements in her students over the school year: "We know our own history, nobody has to tell us, we know it. And they're developing a sense of pride. And I can see it's taken a long time, but it's happening slowly" (Wells et al. 1999, 12). At one charter school in a Latino community, the founder explained that one of the motivating forces behind the effort to start the school was the way Latino students whose English proficiency was limited were being treated in public schools:

> Some of our students who were not English speaking, who were getting close to fluency but not quite there yet, many of them were put in ESL [English as a Second Language] programs. And sometimes the kids never progressed out of ESL, you know, they just continued at the junior high and high school level. And [one of the school's founders] had been at a junior high where she saw the kinds of classes where some of the students wound up. They wound up in huge classes and they worked straight out of grammar books, and she just felt there could be another kind of program for these kids. (Wells et al. 1999, 17)

Many parents have started parent-led charter schools in which a core of extremely devoted and involved parents works with educators to move toward charter school status and is intricately involved in the writing of policies and procedures for the charters. Most of these parent-led charter schools are found in wealthy communities in suburban or exclusive urban areas (Wells et al. 1999, 12), and the parents at these schools govern the school, raise money through private fund-raisers, do volunteer work, and help the school define the terms of the financial and legal agreements.

Frustration among parents has also led to the creation of home-schooling charter schools. Under this arrangement, home-schooling advocates draw together under one charter "umbrella," and each umbrella is usually made up of a cluster of families and parents that have been home schooling their children prior to the creation of the charter school. Motivations for home-schooling charters can vary, but they include religious, practical, pedagogical, and philosophical reasons. The families that are associated with a charter and operate as home-schoolers under a district school charter can run the political gamut from the extremely conservative to the more progressive. A home-schooling charter school does not force parents to adopt any particular formula, ideology, or curriculum; parents make their own pedagogical decisions as to what they wish to adopt as instructional methods and techniques. Still, it is important to remember that they are subject to accountability under state educational standards.

Generally, the majority of the home-schooling students and parents enrolled in the home-schooling charter schools are white and, for the most part, middle class (Wells et al. 1999, 13), and it is usually the nonworking mothers who do the instructing. As a result, those families or parents that home-school typically have the time and economic resources to take advantage of the freedom from the traditional public school system.

A lack of educational innovation, dehumanization, discrimination on the basis of race or socioeconomic class, inadequate teaching strategies, fear of school violence, and lack of input into the control and authority of curriculum and school affairs have all combined to create parental frustration with the current traditional public schools. And parents are not alone in their frustration.

Teacher Frustration

Many teachers also experience deep frustration with the current public school system, and numerous charter schools have emerged from the dreams of educational leaders and teachers who want to do things differently. Teachers encounter intense bureaucracy, increasing levels of paperwork, and time-consuming clerical duties. Many argue that their schools offer no educational leadership, lack a vision of what students should be doing and what they should know, and fail to adopt innovation and creativity as the cornerstone for educational reform and improvement. Many teachers argue that the large public schools are unnecessarily bureaucratic and unresponsive and simply cannot meet the challenges of educating the nation's children. Along with parents, teachers argue that the inordinate class sizes they are forced to handle make teaching and learning difficult and often impossible tasks.

These frustrations are not confined to urban schools, for a national study of rural schools found that those schools experienced similar problems. Despite their smaller class sizes, the study found that the rural schools studied seemed to encourage and foment a bureaucratic style of governing and thinking, thus creating impersonal relationships—from the classroom to the lunchroom.

In *Chartering Urban Reform*, Michelle Fine quotes an urban high school teacher:

> It was "do your own thing" before charters. Teachers rarely shared their strategies and programs. Meetings were all administrative, no pedagogy going on. In charters with colleagues, in department or interdisciplinary meetings, there's a lot more strategizing. There was no opportunity to talk to my colleagues before. There was no reason to talk to colleagues before. Teaching interdisciplinarily, it's compulsory. I am certainly learning from colleagues, and colleagues ask me for help. Last week a teacher who has never in 35 years of teaching broken his class into groups, did so. He's not [even] in a charter. (Fine 1994a, 7)

Much like the parental frustration discussed earlier, teachers find that impersonal administrations coupled with inadequate teaching strategies have reduced the effectiveness of public schools. They point to the lack of educational and professional growth opportunities. One teacher in a charter in Philadelphia recently noted: "I always thought of myself as a good teacher; but not always so creative. I have never enjoyed teaching as much as I do now. I am learning from my colleagues in the charter and, the most amazing thing, I never thought my students wanted to see themselves as students! We would all give the class away to the most disruptive students. Now the students tell Charlie to 'shut up and let us learn'" (Fine 1994a, 11). As once expressed by the noted educator Henry Giroux, teachers want to be treated as professionals and intellectuals in the classroom, not as clerks and technicians (Giroux 1988).

Fine, in studying high schools in the urban America, found that what she called *silencing* occurred at the high schools she studied. This silencing was, according to Fine, the inability to engage student thinking on major controversial issues they faced. As she noted in 1988:

> Now I work with this major urban restructuring effort. By dismantling large anonymous bureaucratic structures of high school, educators and parents are inventing educator-designed, parent-involved, and student-empowered communities of learning called *charters*. Through my work with these high school educators, parents and students and work with Chicago, New York and Baltimore reform, I have come to see how thoroughly *silencing* defines life inside public education bureaucracies. The risks attached to speaking aloud, raising critique, voicing possibility, questioning traditional practices, and challenging social injustices are felt to be enormous. In many major cities, educators echo horror stories about what happens if you are not "loyal." The adverse consequences can be devastating. (Fine 1994b, 81)

Charter schools have also given teachers a new respect for the students they teach. Commenting about her experience with students in a charter school in Philadelphia, one teacher stated that in a charter school,

> you get to know more about kids—everything including their blood type. When you thought about it, there we were with kids from 7:47 to 2:46—all those hours, four years, and *nothing*. It had to be wrong. Knowing a smaller group of students intimately has to change our relationship with them. The charter structure was a place in which we could change and accept our share of the responsibility for student achievement and failure. (Vanderslice and Farmer 1994, 89)

Another teacher, commenting on her new understanding of the students she teaches and the lives they live, noted with some fear:

> OK, Michele, you told me you wanted to get to know these kids. Now we do. And we know what is going on with them. The kid that used to flash the lights on and off in the back of the room isn't just a discipline problem, he's a young man with a crack-addicted mother, or she is homeless. These students have hard lives. Other than taking them home, I don't know what to do with them. You need to get me some help. (Vanderslice and Farmer 1994, 89)

For many teachers, charter schools have given them an opportunity to understand the larger society within which they operate and the Dickensian lives that many of their students are forced to live.

For quite some time, teachers have mourned the lack of cooperative planning time they have together. In many charter schools, where there is an opportunity to discuss everyday interactions between themselves and students, teachers sometimes take risks with their students, share power with their colleagues, and confront the consequences of isolation and disempowerment that are part of many large school districts. Many teachers have found that collaboration is enhanced in charter schools. One high school teacher in Philadelphia noted the problems associated with collaboration among staff members:

> Thinking that the most workable pair [for team teaching purposes] would be English and world history, I asked the history teacher, the long-term substitute, to do an interdisciplinary unit with me; he agreed ... I kept a journal, elicited written responses, to questions from my partner, and got journals and test results from the students. These pieces of writing show me that the students benefited greatly from the synergy of the collaboration. They also show that our collaboration was unequal, that most of the problems that occurred were solved by one person, that the expectations both of each other and of the students varied, and that the perception of the need for the structure was different for each teacher. Problems with collaborating remain. The type and amount of planning needed must be negotiated at the beginning of the partnership. I feel that we were very far apart on this issue. In my next collaboration, at the beginning, I will insist that we negotiate how often we meet, who calls the meetings and what we should get accomplished at the meeting. (Lytle et al. 1994, 176–177)

For many teachers, charter schools offer an opportunity to forge collaborations that previously did not exist. By creating and delivering education in small, intensive units with low ratios of teachers to students and plenty of opportunities to forge relationships among colleagues, many teachers argue that they, for the first time, now have the opportunity to use a wide range of instructional techniques, collaborate successfully with colleagues, create individualized instruction, and upgrade the general quality of their instruction.

Here are just some of the comments offered by teachers at various charter schools about the opportunities those schools afforded them:

> You see someone with a rigid teaching style who's not yet open to a variety of kids' learning styles. But there is no room (in traditional schools) for repair *through* collaboration.

When we meet as a team to talk about students, we can brainstorm on how to handle problems. It makes a great deal of difference when I can say to that student, "Well your other teachers said *this* about you." We are working as a team and students *know* that.

I'm more aware of who their other teachers are and what they're doing. I tell students to *watch how their teachers teach*. That can help students study.

It's better for individual teachers because theirs is not the only viewpoint on a student or class. They get ideas on how to handle a class because everyone has the same group.

Our idea was creating a safe place, an atmosphere of acceptance. There's no anonymity in a charter—that's why insecure teachers avoid them. Vulnerabilities hang out. That's where the charter is good because then vulnerabilities are accepted and teachers start developing strengths to start overcoming those vulnerabilities. In dealing with students holistically, as we can in the charter, we are dealing with teachers holistically as well. (Fine 1994a, 12)

One teacher at a charter high school offered: "Finally I can teach students in ways that allow me to engage with them and other faculty, and hold onto them for their entire secondary school experience" (Fine 1994a, 10). Yet another teacher, who was also a charter coordinator in Philadelphia, described the experience:

Being in a charter, especially with the social work interns, has changed all of my work. So I, and other teachers, are being advocates for students. I was so delighted to hear my principal say, "academics have to drive the rosters, not rosters driving the academics." That's a major change. One more thing: with charters, parents are really involved. We invited 22 parents in for a Family Night, 17 showed up. (Fine 1994a, 11)

One of the results of the increasing teacher frustration with traditional public education has been the development of teacher-led charter schools. These schools are started by groups of teachers who tend to focus on the type of instructional techniques and the instructional programs they feel are important as their primary motivation for going to charter status. They generally are motivated by an educational philosophy and strongly held convictions as to how students should learn. Running the gamut from progressive to multi-age, from open classrooms to more traditional programs, these teacher-led charter schools are built on the idea that teachers know what is best for the students they serve. In these educational settings, the teachers are attempting to gain control of the pedagogy and curriculum in order to develop effective learning and teach in the interest of the student. These schools often become sites of innovation and imagination.

One example of a teacher-initiated charter school is the Constellation Community Middle School in Long Beach, California. This school was started by two public middle-school teachers who felt frustrated because of an inability to change the traditional educational system. Wanting to give their mostly minority students a world-class education, these teachers felt that the charter school idea provided them a way to put restructuring into practice.

Another group of teachers did the same thing at the Sierra Leone Educational Outreach Academy in Detroit, Michigan. This group was composed of former special education teachers who were opposed to the conventional "dumping ground" aspect of traditional special education programs, and they started their own school; just another example of frustration on the part of teachers being translated into teacher-led charter schools.

Even though charter school teachers vary from site to site in terms of their educational philosophy and curriculum orientation, a Hudson Institute study of teachers' personal fulfillment and professional rewards found that over 90 percent of the charter school teachers are "very" or "somewhat" satisfied with their charter school's educational philosophy, size, fellow teachers, and students. The study also found that over 75 percent of the teachers interviewed are satisfied with their school's administration, level of teacher decision making, and the challenge of starting a new school. Only 2.7 percent of charter school teachers say they "hope to be elsewhere" in the future (Hudson Institute 1997, pt. 1, 2).

Although some of the teacher-led charter schools have been started with the help of teachers' union affiliates such as the National Teachers Association, others have been independently started by a handful or a group of teachers. Much like employee-owned companies, these teacher-led charter schools are supportive of public education in general. Their concern is making decisions and judgments as to educational philosophy and corresponding curriculum and instructional tactics in the best interest of the students they teach.

Student Frustration

Students also declare their frustrations with public schools as they are traditionally organized. Students have continually expressed dissatisfaction with everything from school violence to school curriculum. Patterns of frustration can be detected among students throughout the nation from the elementary schools to the high schools.

Students at one charter school in Philadelphia described their frustrations at the failure of traditional education to promote confidence in learning. One high school student noted: "If I were asked in tenth grade whether I was going to college, I would have given a straight 'no.' I was never one who tried to do or accomplish anything. I know now I have abilities. . . . The school has changed me. I feel as though if I study criminal justice, I can probably make a change" (Cohen 1994, 98).

Many students observe that within large, depersonalized, and factory-type schools, their teachers do not care about them or have the confidence that they will learn. For many students, teachers do not have faith in their students at all, and yet, as Asa Hilliard has argued:

> The risk for our children in school is not a risk associated with their intelligence. Public school failures have nothing to do with poverty, race, language, style, and nothing to do with children's families. All of these are red herrings. When researchers study them, we may ultimately yield to some greater insight into the instructional process. But at present, these issues, as explanations of school failure, distract attention away from the fundamental problem facing us today. We have one primary problem: Do we truly see each and every child in this nation develop to the peak of his or her capacities? (Hilliard 1991, 31–35)

Charter schools, argue proponents, offer these students and their teachers opportunities to personalize learning, develop relationships, and examine assumptions about learning and scholastic ability. Such schools offer a systematic change that might allow teachers to develop more respect for their students as they begin to interact with them in a more personal way.

At one high school in Brooklyn, New York, the following were just some of the frustrations with the traditional public school expressed by its urban students:

- ↝ Officials are more interested in impressing students' parents than addressing school problems such as violence
- ↝ Gangs are taking over the hallways
- ↝ Cultural history fails to be acknowledged
- ↝ Teachers don't care
- ↝ Administrators don't serve students
- ↝ Standards need to be higher
- ↝ Classes are too crowded

➥ Curriculum is boring and repetitive. (Sarah J. Hale High School Students 1999, 14)

Such frustrations, like those of teachers and parents, are serving to bolster calls for smaller charter schools. For some students, their experience with charter schools has been an educational lifesaver. A Hudson Institute study of charter schools found that when charter school students were asked what they liked about their charter school, the most frequent answers were "good teachers," 58.6 percent; "they teach until I learn it," 51.3 percent; "and "they don't let me fall behind," 38.5 percent (Hudson Institute 1997, pt. 1, 2). The study also found that when the students' teachers were compared to the teachers in their previous school, three students out of five surveyed (60.7 percent) said that their charter teachers were "better" (Hudson Institute 1997, pt. 1, 2).

Another issue motivating both students and teachers toward charter schools is the importance of personalized learning. Students, like teachers, argue that large class sizes depersonalize learning and fail to allow the necessary time for teacher-student relationships to develop and flourish. Many teachers do not even know the names of some of their students. One high school student in Philadelphia commented on the personalized learning of the smaller class size: "We're in the ninth grade. We should act more mature. We need to make the groups [learning groups] smaller. You get more answers and questions from the girls like Sonia and them" (Waff 1994, 199).

Because charter schools are usually small, they offer opportunities for teachers and students to form relationships that translate into personalized, relevant learning. For example, a student I shall call "Susan" benefited greatly from school choice. In the bottom 25 percent of her regular high school class and undergoing therapy for depression, she was allowed to attend the University of Minnesota special program where her university grade point average was 3.2 percent compared to her high school grade point average of 1.78 percent (all of these examples are from letters sent to Daryl Sedio at the University of Minnesota). "Sam" attended the University of Minnesota special program after having dropped out of high school where he felt he never "fit in." Although his high school grades were D+/C-, he maintained a B+/A- average in the university program.

"Paul" was in the fifty-ninth percentile of his high school class, but when he was allowed to attend the University of Minnesota program, his grades averaged 4.0. "Jon," described as a disruptive, hostile, and highly argumentative individual, failed seven of his eight classes in high school before he dropped out. Nine months later, after starting in the Minnesota program, he was earning an average grade of A while taking courses in philosophy, English, and political science. Two unnamed girls had set the record for absences from their high school, but when they transferred to a nontraditional program outside their district, they planned to not only graduate from high school but also to go on to postsecondary institutions.

As more and more students continue to experience overcrowded classrooms, unsafe schools, repetitive and boring classes, and lack of educational innovation, the impetus among students for charter schools will remain strong.

CONCLUSION

Charter schools remain very popular with their primary constituents. The driving force to create a charter school arises from very different quarters and is motivated by varying and diverse interests. Families and educators seek out charter schools for primarily educational reasons: high academic standards, small class size, a focus on teaching and learning, educational philosophies that are close to their own, and designing innovative approaches to curriculum and instruction are all reasons shared by parents, teachers, and students who have embraced the charter school movement.

REFERENCES

Anderson, J. "Parent Involvement in a Charter School." Paper presented at the annual meeting of the American Educational Research Association, Chicago, 24–28 March 1997.

Brighouse, Harry. "March of the Vouchers." *Against the Current* (September–October 1999).

Carnegie Foundation. *School Choice.* Princeton, NJ: 1992.

Cobb, Casey, and Gene Glass. "Ethnic Segregation in Arizona Charter Schools." *Education Policy Analysis Archives* (peer-reviewed scholarly electronic journal) 7, no. 1 (14 January 1999).

Cohen, J. "Now Everybody Wants to Dance." In M. Fine, *Chartering Urban School Reform,* 98. New York: Columbia University Teachers College, 1994.

Collins, P. H. *Black Feminist Thought: Knowledge, Consciousness, and the Politics of Empowerment.* New York: Routledge, 1991.

Fine, M. *Chartering Urban School Reform: Reflections of Public High Schools in the Midst of Change.* New York: Columbia University Teachers College, 1994a.

———. "Silencing, Inquiry, and Reflection in Public School Bureaucracies." In *Chartering Urban School Reform,* 81. New York: Columbia University Teachers College, 1994b.

Friedman, M. "The Voucher Idea." *New York Times Magazine,* 23 September 1973.

Giroux, Henry. *Teachers as Intellectuals: Toward a Critical Pedagogy of Learning.* Granby, MA: Bergin and Garvey, 1988.

Hassel, Bryan C. *The Charter School Challenge: Avoiding the Pitfalls, Fulfilling the Promise.* Washington, DC: Brookings Institute, 1999.

Hilliard, A. "Do We Have the Will to Educate All Children?" *Educational Leadership* (September 1991): 31–35.

Hudson Institute. *Charter Schools in Action Project.* Final Report, pts. 1 and 6. Washington, DC, 1997.

Hughes, T. J. "Magnets' Pull Weakens in Suburbs." *St. Louis Post Dispatch,* 25 February 1988.

Kolderie, Ted. *The States Begin to Withdraw the Exclusive.* Public Services Redesign Project. St. Paul, MN: Center for Policy Studies, 1993.

Kozol, J. *Death at an Early Age.* Boston: Houghton and Mifflin, 1967.

Lytle, S., J. Christman, J. Cohen, J. Countryman, B. Fecho, D. Portnoy, and F. Sion. "Learning in the Afternoon: When Teacher Inquiry Meets School Reform." In M. Fine, *Chartering Urban School Reform,* 157–80. New York: Columbia University Teachers College, 1994.

Massey, D., and N. A. Denton. *American Apartheid: Segregation and the Making of the Underclass.* Cambridge, MA: Harvard University Press, 1993.

Nathan, Joe. *Charter Schools: Creating Hope and Opportunity for American Education.* San Francisco: Jossey-Bass, 1996.

———. "Early Lessons of the Charter School Movement." *Educational Leadership* 54, no. 2 (October 1996): 19–21.

Saks, Judith B. *The Basics of Charter Schools: A School Board Primer.* Alexandria, VA: National School Boards Association, 1997.

———. "Education Commission of the States' Task Force on Education and Economic Growth." In *Action for Excellence.* Denver: Education Commission of the States, 1983.

Sarah J. Hale High School Students. "Crossing Swords." *Journal of the Society for Social Analysis* 7, no. 1 (Summer/Fall 1999).

Scherer, M. "Let the Dialogue Begin." *Educational Leadership* 55 (May 1998): 5.

Schwartz, W. "How Well Are Charter Schools Serving Urban and Minority Students?" *ERIC/CUE Digest* 119 (November 1996): 4.

Steel, L., and R. Levine. *Educational Innovation in Multiracial Contexts: The*

Growth of Magnet Schools in American Education. Palo Alto, CA: Prepared for the U.S. Department of Education, 1994.

Summers, A. A., and A. W. Johnson. "Review of the Evidence of the Effects of School-based Management Plans." Paper presented at the conference Improving the Performance of America's Schools: Economic Choices, Washington, DC, 12–13 October 1994.

U.S. Department of Education. *A Nation at Risk.* Washington, DC: National Commission on Excellence in Education, 1983.

——. *The State of Charter Schools: National Study of Charter Schools.* Washington, DC: Office of Educational Research and Improvement, May 1999.

Vanderslice, V., and S. Farmer. "Transforming Ourselves: Becoming an Inquiring Community." In M. Fine, *Chartering Urban School Reform,* 85–97. New York: Columbia University Teachers College, 1994.

Waff, D. "Girl Talk: Creating Community through Social Exchange." In M. Fine, *Chartering Urban School Reform,* 192–201. New York: Columbia University Teachers College, 1994.

Watkins, T. "So You Want to Start a Charter School." *Education Week* 40 (6 September 1995).

Wells, Amy, Alejandra Lopez, Janelle Scott, and Jennifer Jellison Holme. "Charter Schools as Postmodern Paradox: Rethinking Social Stratification in an Age of Deregulated School Choice." *Harvard Educational Review* 69, no. 2 (Summer 1999): 1–28.

Chapter Two

✤ Chronology

LATE 1960s AND EARLY 1970s

Parents and innovative public school educators all over the nation join together to design distinctive educational options, or choices, for students. Metro High School in Chicago, City as School in New York, Parkway in Philadelphia, Marcy Open School in Minneapolis, and St. Paul Open School in St. Paul, Minnesota, give public schoolteachers the chance to create new kinds of schools that make sense for a variety of students. Internships and apprenticeships in communities, site-based decision making, and extensive parental involvement are all features of these new and innovative schools. There are no admission requirements, and the schools are open to a variety of students. These schools are designed by groups of parents, educators, and community members, not by central district offices, and are generally operated at the same per-pupil cost as other, more traditional schools.

MID-1970s

Courts and political leaders are faced with massive public opposition to school busing. Congress allocates millions of dollars to create "magnet schools" as one way of promoting racial integration. These schools offer special, sometimes enhanced, curricula to attract a racially diverse student body. They are designed by central school districts as opposed to groups of parents and educators. These schools have admission tests, and the per-pupil cost is often more than that for neighborhood schools.

LATE 1970s AND EARLY 1980s

Public school districts begin creating schools to which they assign alienated, rebellious, and unsuccessful students. The term "alternative school" is used to describe these schools and is thought to imply a program for troubled students.

1983

The publication *A Nation at Risk* expresses dissatisfaction with schools in the United States, specifically the public schools, and is the catalyst for the development of the charter movement.

Innovative public schools, state to state, find that they do not have the control over budgets and faculties they need. Debates among administrators, parents, and teachers begin over the future operation and control of these new schools.

MID-1980s

The California public alternative school group, Learning Alternative Resource Network (LEARN), develops a proposed bill that responds to issues of control and authority in innovative schools. It stipulates that if thirty or more parents and/or pupils request a new school and the teachers within the district choose to teach in it, and if the operating costs are no more than those of programs with equivalent status for the same pupils, the district "shall establish a public school or program of choice responsive to the request." The proposed bill is never introduced or adopted.

In Minnesota, Governor Rudy Perpich introduces proposals for several public school choice programs. His 1985 proposals are strongly supported by an unusual coalition that includes the Minnesota Parent-Teachers Association, directors of the War on Poverty agencies in Minnesota, individual teachers, administrators, and parents, and the Minnesota Business Partnership (MBP).

1988

The Minnesota legislature adopts key parts of Governor Perpich's proposal. The postsecondary option adopted by the legislature allows public high school juniors and seniors to take all or part of their coursework in colleges and universities. The option to attend other public schools is included in the adoption by the legislature. Known as the Areas Learning Center Law and High School Graduation Incentive Act, this law, which passed in 1987, allows teenagers and adults who have not previously succeeded in school to attend public schools outside their district boundaries. The bill also allows students to attend private, nonsectarian schools if a local district contracts with those schools.

The open enrollment portion of the legislation is passed in 1988 and allows students from kindergarten through twelfth grade to apply to attend public schools outside their districts as long as the receiving district has room and the transfer does not increase racial segregation. This becomes the first real state experience with choice programs, and these programs begin to receive publicity and support throughout the United States.

Ray Budde, a retired teacher and expert on school district reorganization, proposes that a school board directly charter teams of teachers to establish new, innovative programs within a district for a three- to five-year period. His book, *Education by Charter: Restructuring School Districts*, begins the first public debate regarding charter schools.

In an address at a Minneapolis conference on improving public schools, American Federation of Teachers president Albert Shanker supports the idea of giving teachers a chance to create innovative new programs and charter schools and goes even further to suggest the creation of entire new schools. He suggests that both the school board and the majority of teachers working in a school be required to approve the new school. On 31 March, Shanker makes a speech to the National Press Club in Washington, D.C., in which he endorses these ideas again.

The 1988 annual convention of the American Federation of Teachers endorses the charter school idea at the urging of Shanker. Paying tribute to Budde's idea, Shanker advocates that local school boards and teachers' unions jointly develop a procedure to enable teams of teachers to establish autonomous public schools within school buildings. He calls these schools within schools "charter schools."

EARLY 1990s

The accountability movement in education, deregulation, decentralization, the movement toward on-site management, local control issues, restructuring of schools, issues of teacher empowerment, and discussions of more local district control all contribute to the charter school movement.

The growing threat of private school vouchers propels the charter movement to the forefront in an effort to provide choice within a public school context. Charters are seen as a compromise by adhering to the idea of public education while embracing competion and other free market principles.

1991

Minnesota becomes the first state to pass charter school legislation. The law is limited in scope, authorizing no more than eight charter schools statewide, and requires that local school boards approve each charter. The original law is later amended to permit forty charter schools and allow the state board of education, upon appeal, to authorize a charter school after a local district has turned it down.

1992

California passes legislation that allows up to 100 charter schools in the state.

1993

Colorado and Massachusetts pass strong charter school laws.

1994

Eleven states have legislation that allows charter schools. A federal Public Charter Schools Program is made law as part of the 1994 amendments to the Elementary and Secondary Education Act. The program is designed to help charter schools in states where they are legally allowed.

1995

Eight more states pass charter school legislation (Alaska, Arkansas,

Delaware, Louisiana, New Hampshire, Rhode Island, Texas, and Wyoming).

1996

Connecticut, Florida, Illinois, New Jersey, North Carolina, and South Carolina pass charter school legislation, and the movement begins to gain real momentum throughout the United States.

In October, Secretary of Education Richard Riley announces the award of $17 million in the form of grants to seventeen states and Puerto Rico and the District of Columbia to support the start-up and development of hundreds of additional charter schools.

1997

Pennsylvania and Mississippi pass charter legislation; seven states, including Virginia and Nevada, turn down similar legislation.

The U.S. Congress increases federal funding for the Public Charter Schools Program to $51 million in fiscal 1997, and President Clinton asks the congressional appropriations committees to double the funding to $100 million by 1998.

By the summer, nearly 500 charter schools are operating in twenty-seven states and the District of Columbia.

1998

By the end of 1998, thirty-four states and the District of Columbia have passed charter school legislation.

1999–2000

The Center for Education Reform reports that 1,682 charter schools will open their doors to approximately 350,000 children in thirty-one states and the District of Columbia for the current school year.

Chapter Three

◆ Curriculum and Instructional Approaches

Because there are so many questions regarding the efficacy of charter schools, this chapter explores the diverse curriculum and varied instructional and philosophical approaches that some charter schools are pursuing. These curriculum and instructional approaches vary from school to school—reflecting the diverse educational philosophies that underlie the curriculum approaches of the various schools. A brief and general overview of the curriculum approaches and instructional philosophies of some of these schools will provide an insight into how many of them construct their educational designs and curriculum. Both urban and rural charter schools in various states will be discussed.

A GENERAL LOOK AT WHAT SOME CHARTER SCHOOLS ARE DOING

Preserving Native-American Heritage

At the Blackwater Charter School located on the Gila River Indian Reservation south of Phoenix, Arizona, Gilbert Innis, the tribal education director of the Gila River community, says that charter schools have allowed tribal officials to emphasize the tribe's history, language, and customs as well as to prepare its children for the future. Teachers utilize words from the tribe's heritage in their lessons, and the people of the reservation believe they have been able to take direction of the school in an attempt to preserve their culture.

The curriculum at the four schools that compose the Gila educational system is based on tribal heritage and reflects tribal concerns. For example, history, social science, and science lessons include discussions about the tribe and how the tribe has evolved over time. Besides teaching the O'otham language, the charter school curriculum includes hands-on learning, such as gardening, to teach about crops and the tribe's historical heritage. Future plans call for the inclusion of an archeological site where the students will be able to dig for pottery shards like those crafted by their ancestors.

Years ago, if Native Americans in Arizona used their native language, that was a punishable offense in the Bureau of Indian Affairs reservation schools and boarding schools for Native Americans. Now, the situation is reversed. Whereas members of the Gila tribe were once encouraged to learn English and white ways of knowing at the expense of their own cultural heritage and identity, they are now stimulated and animated to reconnect with their past through a curriculum based on cultural heritage. The charter school concept affords them an opportunity to reconnect the tribe's educational process to what it values as a people.

Oakland Charter Academy

Located in Oakland, California, the Oakland Charter Academy, formerly known as Jingletown, is a junior high school committed to bilingual and multicultural education. The school, which derived its earlier name from the East Oakland neighborhood where most of the families of the students are from, began operation in 1993, and six years later it was serving 190 students in the seventh through the ninth grades. This academy grew out of the organizational efforts of Latino parents and a committed principal who felt that lower class sizes, block scheduling for core subjects, cooperative learning, bilingual education, and multicultural education should be the cornerstones of a progressive education. The school values the Chicano heritage and bilingual instruction and is committed to fostering a learning environment that provides for development and continuous lifelong learning.

According to the principal of the school, Clementina Duron, the organizing effort came about as a result of a coalition of parents at Lazear Elementary School who wanted bilingual educational opportunities for their children (*Rethinking Schools* 1996, 10). They were impressed by the success of bilingual education in the elementary school and wanted this type of education to continue throughout the junior high school and high school experiences. Parents and community members argued in 1993 that although bilingual education was mandated by the state for students whose English proficiency was limited there were few schools with bilingual teachers and a commitment to educational excellence through instruction in a student's native language. Parents wanted to see their children learn English without sacrificing their native language, and these parents and community members felt the need for a school that would respond to the needs of working-class Latino students, who, they argued, were underserved by the traditional education programs. The parents also felt the traditional public schools were impersonal and beset by violence and gangs. They felt that their children's educational opportunities were in jeopardy, and this belief, coupled with California's charter legislation, formed the impetus for the development of the school.

Yet when Duron joined with parents and community members to start the charter school in 1993, they faced open hostility from the district school board and the teachers' union (Wallis 1994). The district refused to allow the proposed school to participate in the district's self-insurance program, which would have cost only $400 as opposed to the $10,000 that Duron and community members had to pay for private liability insurance. Nor was the district willing to share its legal services or the services of its payroll department. According to Duron, the district's attitude could be summed up as: "You guys want to run your own school, then you do the whole thing. Go ahead and fall on your faces" (Wallis 1994).

Despite the open hostility of the district, the parents, community, and Duron persisted and persevered. On 20 August 1993, three weeks before the scheduled beginning of the school year, the district approved the opening of Jingletown. The local Roman Catholic diocese provided a small park as a temporary site, and during the weeks that followed, parents dug ditches for electrical and sewage lines in a feverish effort to begin the school on time. They rented eight portable classrooms for the school's initial 120 students. When the classes did finally begin, the sewage lines still had not been completed and according to Duron: "For three weeks, kids had nowhere to go to the bathroom. We had to knock on doors in the neighborhood. I'd take kids ten at a time" (Wallis 1994).

The educational focus of the Oakland Charter Academy is based on Latino historical and cultural awareness and the preservation of the native language. When the school was initially created, the educational priorities set forth in the charter proposal were smaller classroom size, two-hour blocks for core-subject teaching, bilingual and multicultural instruction, cooperative learning, and diversity of the teaching staff. The majority of the teachers at the school are Latino and bilingual, and they are either activist in nature or believe in progressive educational approaches.

A Curriculum Designed by Children

One teacher with thirty years of experience, Elaine Young of Westchester, New York, has submitted a preliminary application for a unique charter school. Her idea is to have the curriculum designed by the children and be based on their interests. Hoping that the school can open in September 2001, Young envisions classrooms that she calls "exploratorium." In an interview for the local paper, the *Westchester Weekly Desk,* Young stated:

> The vision is to have the children involved in the design of their own learning based on their interests, because jobs are not what they used to be. The world is project based, team-based, flexible. The children would be involved in the planning, design, and setup of the school, and it would be a very demanding inquiry process throughout the grades, and the children will demonstrate and see a use for the skills, knowledge and information that we want them to know and how it is applied to life. We still have to meet the standards of New York State. (Greene 1999, 2)

Young is a proponent of discovery and constructionist learning, and the opportunity to open a school designed by students is exciting and stimulating because it gives her and her students a chance to learn based on a shared curriculum. She plans on basing her curriculum on a relevant, hands-on discovery approach to learning, and she wants the school to be able to offer students the ability to see how the knowledge and information they are acquiring can be useful in their daily lives. By basing the curriculum on a project-based approach to learning designed by and for students, Young is hoping to offer an environment in which students can "learn to love what they learn and learn what they love" (Greene 1999, 1).

Alianza Bilingual Immersion Model

At the Alianza School, located in Santa Cruz County near the Monterey Bay Sanctuary in California, the mission "is to teach understanding and respect for racial, cultural and linguistic diversity. This is accomplished through our Two Way Bilingual Immersion Program for all students which emphasizes academic achievement, acquisition of a second language, cooperation with others and the appreciation of each individual's uniqueness" (Alianza School website).

The school is committed to teaching all of its 650 students in kindergarten through sixth grade the ability to speak a second language. The two-way bilingual immersion program means that all students, regardless of their native language, learn their basic skills in Spanish. In kindergarten, they spend 90 percent of the day with a teacher who uses Spanish as the primary language in the classroom, and 10 percent of the day is spent with an English-speaking teacher. As the students move up through the grade levels, the percentage of English-language exposure increases until by the fourth grade, instruction is 50 percent in English and 50 percent in Spanish. In kindergarten, the English portion of the day focuses on language skills; by the fifth and sixth grades, English instruction includes not only language and literacy skills but also mathematics, science, fine arts, and physical education. All teachers learn effective bilingual teaching strategies through a program made possible by a government (Title VII) grant.

Located in a rural section of California, 90 percent of the students are Latino and primarily of Mexican heritage. There is a 55 percent migrant population, 60 percent of the students are English language learners, and the English proficiency of at least 51 percent of the school's 1,000 students is limited. The school faced potential disaster when the state of California passed Proposition 227 in 1998, for that measure abolished bilingual education in the state and mandated English-only programs. Fearing that the school's two-way bilingual immersion program would be destroyed, Alianza chose instead to become a charter school and thus circumvent the proposition. Michael Jones, principal at Alianza, stated: "If there is a silver lining in Proposition 227, it is that people are going to have to be very clear about what their programs are about. Parents who are signing a waiver (to demand bilingual education) must want their kids to be truly biliterate and truly bilingual" (Miner 1999, 12).

Alianza initially started in 1980 as a magnet school tied to a voluntary desegregation plan (Miner 1999, 19). It has always offered bilingual instruction to its students, and in the early 1990s, the staff began discussions to determine how they might improve the program. In 1993, the school began to implement its two-way immersion program, and since that time, and with the passage of Proposition 227, the school has made a successful transition to charter school status and now offers its unique two-way immersion program to students and the community.

For Alianza, the transition has meant developing an educational philosophy of biliteracy within the charter school rubric. It has also meant the development of dual immersion—sometimes referred to as two-way immersion. The concept is simple: students who are dominant in English sit alongside students who are dominant in Spanish, and together, they learn each others' language. At the time of this writing, the district had announced that it will open another neighborhood elementary school with a bilingual program and that Alianza will become a district-wide choice school while maintaining both its charter status and its two-way immersion program.

A Back-to-Basics Charter School

Specializing in individual instruction and priding itself on being a back-to-basics school, the San Diego Charter School is located in forty-four storefront classrooms in eighteen different locations throughout San Diego, California. Students develop and work with individualized education plans that may include in-class work, and the students move at their own pace through an instructional design model based on independent study (Charter School of San Diego website).

Sponsored by the San Diego Chamber of Commerce and the city's Business Roundtable for Education, the Charter School of San Diego was formalized as a school on 1 July 1994. At that time, it was the city's newest secondary school, and it grew dramatically with the help of a complex system of community partnerships and alliances. The charter school now operates citywide.

The Charter School of San Diego bases its course of study and curriculum on state frameworks that spell out what standards students are expected to achieve. Although the standards may comprise the curriculum focus and objective, the method of instruction at the Charter School of San Diego is anything but conventional.

The school seeks to serve students who are convinced they will not achieve academically. As a result, the school places its emphasis on individualized instruction, unique teacher-student relationships, the involvement of parents, and the small community setting of the schools. Instruction is offered individually or in the form of small group seminars. Teachers teach interdisciplinarily. Classes run from morning to night, and students take one or two courses at a time. Even the calendars and schedules are personalized and individualized for students.

Both parents and teachers play important roles at the school. Both help develop school policy and give regular feedback at various and frequently scheduled meetings.

A SPECIFIC LOOK AT WHAT SOME CHARTER SCHOOLS ARE DOING

Freire Charter School

The Freire Charter School in Philadelphia opened on 7 September 1999 with 110 eighth-grade students and plans to add a grade each year through grade twelve. The school's physical space, equipment, cleaning, and security service are provided by Temple University in Philadelphia.

The school's students are 85 percent African American, and the remaining 15 percent is split between Caucasians and Latinos. Of the ten teachers at Freire, four are black, one is Latino, and five are white (interview with Jay Guben, 14 March 2000).

The Freire Charter School attempts to offer a blend of academic and experiential learning. In an interview with Jay Guben, the school's founder, he indicated to me that the school uses experiential learning mixed with the philosophy of the Brazilian educator Paolo Freire. Emphasizing individualized, self-directed learning, the school requires individualized learning plans from its students. These plans are designed to offer a focus and unite students with the resources they will need to complete their learning, such as teachers, mentors, parents, community members, and employers.

Educational Focus

Freire's curriculum and programming, which are notable for their extraordinary quality and depth, include features such as:

- A small learning community
- A student-teacher ratio of 18 to 1
- A mentor for every student
- Community service, work experience, and entrepreneurial training
- Research and evaluation combined with student reflection and analysis
- Individual learning plans
- Structured, ongoing parental involvement and learning programs for parents
- A computer in every student's home
- A core commitment to making Freire's learning program work, based upon the considered choice of its students, parents, faculty, and administration that Freire is where they want to be

The school envisions a progressive education for young people. Its vision is comprehensive and speaks to what the school is trying to accomplish and what it sees as education for democracy. Further, the vision statement provides a theoretical understanding of the school's day-to-day practice—why the school is structured as it is, why the curriculum is constructed as it is, the role of learner and teacher, and the collaborative nature of learning. Many schools have mission statements that accompany their charter, usually four or five sentences about what the school seeks to accomplish, but the Freire Charter School goes further to actually envision the educational climate and reality it seeks for students and educational workers. According to Guben, the school is attempting to put forth a philosophy of learning to change the mind-set regarding what schools should be, how they should function, and what should go on within them. In this respect, the Freire Charter School is unique.

The following is the vision statement in its entirety, as first introduced on the school's website:

> What makes Freire Charter School special? Freire Charter School brings to life concepts that everyone agrees are sound. It puts the student at the center of a rich and interconnected set of learning experiences. It structures a range of multi-disciplinary experiential learning in community workplaces and other settings. It makes multiculturalism a living part of the curriculum and communal life. It cares for students through small classes, advisory relationships, and formal mentoring. It governs itself democratically, nurturing and honoring student participation in governance as well as in instruction. It values consensus and accountability. It infuses technology and will provide every student and family with a computer on loan and Internet access at home. It involves families directly in learning—their children's and their own. It partners with successful people and organizations, it aspires to be a joyful community of empowered people.
>
> Learning experiences at Freire are designed by the students, their teachers and their families to address current and future learning needs. Teachers will guide students as they embark on their own search for knowledge. That search focuses students on developing the skills to acquire, assess, and produce knowledge. Freire equips them to grow into strong family members, good neighbors, responsible citizens, lifelong learners, and productive adults.
>
> At Freire, the learning process is part of the outcome. Students engage in real-world activities that make knowledge coherent, connected, memorable, and useful. Coursework at Freire is crafted around problematizing curriculum that emphasizes exploration into "meaningful" issues and problems. Academic courses are challenging. A longer school day and year enable students to engage in hands-on study in a variety of community and workplace settings. Mistakes are valued for their learning potential.
>
> Freire has designed the five-year high school program to begin with 8th grade. This configuration capitalizes on the energy and intellectual curiosity of these young people as it initiates them into a systematic

process for maximizing the development of their interests and capabilities. The five-year program also allows ample time for students to discover and explore diverse options and set priorities, and to take full advantage of the multiplicity of community partnerships that are available to them. For example, at Freire, each student receives a mentor. The mentorship program is sponsored with the school in conjunction with Big Brothers and Big Sisters of America. The mentorship calls for personal contact once per week between mentor and mentoree. The five-year program also eases the transition from elementary to high school.

The five-year curriculum includes a graduated program of applied community experiences with emphasis on team skills and workplace readiness. The first three years involve students in community service and the exploration of careers in commercial institutions and entrepreneurial ventures. The last two years are focused on more intensive research and extended internship in students' given fields. Academic coursework, especially in the last year, is explicitly geared to support and connect to students' emerging career and life goals.

Relationships are paramount at Freire. Freire seeks to be inclusive of cultures and conditions among students and staff. Differences are expected to be acknowledged and respected. Awareness of, and sensitivity to, multiple perspectives infuse relationships and the actual school curriculum.

Organizational Management and Educational Accountability

Freire students will never doubt that they are part of a community of students and at the center of a circle of adults who care about them and their development. The adults include their families, their teachers, and community partners, the last including job-site associates and mentors. These adults are highly accessible to the students in person, by telephone, and on-line.

At the Freire Charter School, internal evaluations are used to measure the school's success, and there are also outside consultants who comment on the school's progress. The school uses authentic assessment, i.e., performance assessment, peer review, and portfolios, to test and develop student performance, and the school also is subject to state standardized testing mechanisms.

In the mentoring program, the mentors are more than just role models. They help provide students with real-life experiences and a hands-on approach in dealing with the experiences. National research by Public/Private Ventures, a national nonprofit organization, has shown that mentoring by Big Brother and Big Sister programs makes it significantly less likely that young people will start using illegal drugs or alcohol, skip a class or a day of school, hit someone, or lie to their parents, and participation in mentoring relationships makes young people more trusting of their parents or guardians and allows them to feel more supported by their peers and friends.

Freire also pursues democratic ideals. Students and adults alike have rights and responsibilities. Students have a voice in designing their studies and demonstrate what they have learned, are active constructors of knowledge and makers of meaning, and participate in evaluating their learning throughout their years at the school. Students are expected to play multiple roles in governance. They not only develop and run a representative student council but they also have seats on the school's board of directors and the school's management team. Students are also invited to join various advisory and decision-making task forces, focus groups, or committees. Staff, families, and community partners also have roles in management and governance.

Learning at Freire is also meant to be fun, and wonder and inquiry are welcomed. The Freire community celebrates many kinds of success. It seeks to develop an expandable body of traditions and celebrations and studies ways to make learning and community life pleasant, rewarding ventures for students and adults.

Professional growth among teachers is also important. Like the students, the teachers must develop an individualized professional growth plan that they will pursue, and the school pays the costs of professional development for the staff. The school does not have a collective bargaining unit, that is, it is not a union school. Teachers have the option to join the state and national teachers' unions, but so far, they have not done so.

Freire is therefore special for many reasons. The students get to make many choices about their own education; they are encouraged to articulate, pursue, and expand their interests; they learn to control powerful technological tools; they develop interpersonal skills they can use in daily life; they work with other students; they share learning with their families; they are equipped to encounter new people and new situations; they make a difference in their communities; and they dream about what they want to become while they actively work toward bringing their dreams to fruition (Freire Charter School website).

In my interview with Jay Guben, he mentioned that the greatest barrier to achieving success is implementing the dream. From his point of view, living up to the promises made to the students, parents, staff, and community remains the biggest challenge. Much like in other public schools, the tension between the students who are at Freire to learn and those who are merely there to escape traditional public schooling remains high. However, for Guben and the Freire Charter School's staff, parents, and students, the promises are great, the hope and optimism are encouraging, and the possibility for success is high.

Minnesota New Country School

The Minnesota New Country School is located in what is called "the valley of the Jolly Green Giant" in LeSueur, Minnesota. This rural school serves about ninety-five students from grades six through twelve. Established by two teachers and the technical director of a small private computer company, the three principal founders wanted to focus attention on the use of new technology in curriculum delivery. Frustrated by the lack of innovation in the traditional public school, Kim Borwege and Nancy Miller, the two teachers responsible for this charter school, went to the local school board to request a charter (Nathan 1996, 35). Although the local school board initially turned them down, the two teachers diligently worked with the community, parents, teachers, and businesses to build support for what eventually became the New Country School.

Miller and Borwege worked with members of the community to put forth a vision of the school they wanted. The mission statement for the school emphasizes a learning community committed to a quality project based on a learning process that is personalized and allows the student to demonstrate achievement. The school is committed to providing an environment in which students can demonstrate strong skills and knowledge prior to graduation, one that makes extensive use of the support of the community, and one that incorporates new technology in its instructional and learning design (Nathan 1996, 35).

Finally, after consistent organizing and the presentation of a plan, the board agreed to grant the school a charter. However, the charter was granted as a "revenue-neutral" charter, which meant the school could not cost the district money, even though dozens of district students were planning to attend. The proponents accepted the charter.

The Minnesota New Country School, like many other charter schools, looks different from most traditional public schools. Its school buildings are former storefronts on the city's Main Street. With the help of parents and community volunteers, the school founders reconstructed the storefronts into classrooms and offices. The school is open from 8:00 a.m. until 5:30 or 6:00 p.m., and students can be seen working there from early in the morning until late in the afternoon. Each Monday evening the school remains open for parents, community members, and staff. And rather than establishing its own food service, the school has a contract with the Main Street Café, a local eating establishment, to provide lunch.

Educational Focus

The Minnesota New Country School does not have classrooms in the traditional sense. Operating out of storefront facilities in the city's downtown, the school is staffed by employee-students. Working with a list of several hundred competencies, from reading to mathematics, the school helps students develop a post–high school plan for their continuing education and/or work, and the school's students and employees work as a team.

The New Country School has a strong vision, as is stated in the teacher/student accountability section of its website:

> MNCS is not interested in the number of minutes or hours a student spends at a desk or works on a particular course. We are interested in each student's ability to achieve at the highest level possible; to reach clearly defined, integrated outcomes; to complete an individual learning plan designed by student, parents and teachers. . . . As members of this team, the teachers understand the awesome responsibility they have to students, parents, communities and those who assist them in any way. (Minnesota New Country School website)

Based on the philosophy of Ted Sizer and the Coalition of Essential Schools, a national movement for public school reform, the Minnesota New Country School advocates that students be thought of as workers, and the school focuses on helping students learn to think critically and to use their minds well. The school also believes that its goal should be simple: to help students master a limited number of skills and areas of knowledge, based on the notion that schools should not attempt to be all-encompassing and comprehensive but should personalize learning around central themes (Minnesota New Country School website, 2).

The school has one computer for every two students, and the students have created their own home page on the computer. Although some students spend time reading and writing on a given day, others have apprenticeships and internships at places such as a local radio station and the chamber of commerce. Field trips, internships, and a hands-on application of knowledge form the core of the school's educational approach.

With small groups developed for learning coupled with low class sizes, teachers can move from student to student assessing progress, asking questions, and reviewing work. Group projects are developed by students, and the groups meet with teachers to review student projects on a continuing basis.

One major school project became the focus of a national inquiry. Taking water samples from the Minnesota River, students noticed that frogs appeared to have two, three, or five legs instead of the traditional four. Looking more closely, they saw that many, if not most, of the frogs had similar mutations. The students contacted the Minnesota Pollution Control Agency, which visited the site and confirmed a serious and potentially grave situation regarding the river's pollution. The story culminated in 1996 when the students testified before the Minnesota legislature. The legislature eventually passed a bill giving thousands of dollars to the Pollution Control Agency for research and study, and these activities were to include the support and work of students from the New Country School (Minnesota New Country School website).

The school also holds conferences with each student and each student's parents in order to solidify the relationship among the students, parents, teachers, and the school. Included in the meetings is the development of individual learning plans on behalf of the students. The staff of the school looks to parents for support and involvement, and by holding planning conferences with both parents and students, the school believes that strong working relationships will develop that will ensure success for the students and provide a bridge between work done at school and work done at home.

Besides the planning sessions, a "presentation night" is held in the community center every two months, and this occasion allows the school and its staff to report student progress. Anyone can attend from the community, and students are asked to make a presentation of their learning to all in attendance. The presentation is videotaped, and feedback is given to the students from the teaching staff.

Organizational Management and Educational Accountability

The Minnesota New Country School is managed through a decentralized, accountable system. Principals and teachers are encouraged to perceive of themselves as generalists first and as specialists second. The school follows the essential principles of educational reformer Ted Sizer, which means that the staff should expect and accept multiple obligations within the school and demonstrate a commitment to the entire school (Minnesota New Country School website).

The administrative and budget targets mandate substantial time for collective planning by teachers, competitive salaries for staff, and an ultimate per-pupil cost that is not to exceed that of traditional schools by more than 10 percent (Minnesota New Country School website). Because the school was to be revenue-neutral, the school received start-up grants from several sources in order to obtain the necessary learning equipment. And because the school's teachers decided to do away with an administrator, they were able to save thousands of dollars that were then used for such things as technology and higher salaries. Teachers were also able to develop their own working conditions, such as the length of the teaching day.

In order to evaluate student progress with respect to state standards, record keeping is a time-consuming activity. Yearly evaluations coupled with personal growth plans on the part of students allow both teachers and students to document and report student progress. Simultaneously, each teacher develops a personal growth plan that is reviewed periodically by an evaluation committee of the board. The committee reviews each teacher's growth plan and provides feedback.

O'Farrell Community School

One of the first districts in California to sponsor charter schools, San Diego is the eighth-largest urban district in the nation, and its experiences with charter schools highlight many of the complex issues that face such schools and the districts that approve them. Of the 133,000 schoolchildren the district educates, 16.8 percent are African American, 34 percent are Hispanic, 8.1 percent are Filipino, 7.1 percent are Indochinese (Vietnamese, Cambodian, and Laotian), 2.5 percent are Asian (Chinese, Japanese, and Korean), and 29 percent are Caucasian. At the time of writing, San Diego had six charter schools serving a total of 4,500 students, or 3.4 percent of the total school population within the district (Council of Urban Boards 1997, 29).

The charter schools have elected to participate together in what might be considered a formal consortium, and they hold regular self-help and technical workshops with the assistance of the San Diego Chamber of Commerce Business Roundtable for Education. One of the issues the San Diego charter schools have faced is whether a charter school can be considered a separate legal entity from the district that charters it. This controversy came to light with a debate surrounding the Johnson Elementary School.

San Diego's Urban League had collaborated with the Johnson Elementary School to convert the school to charter status. The Urban League and the city had been at odds for nearly two decades over desegregation and student performance, and changing the status of the Johnson Elementary School was an attempt to upgrade the academic achievement of San Diego's African American students. However, in 1996, the board voted unanimously to revoke the charter, arguing that the school had broken California state law by retaining its own legal counsel and asserting its legal independence from the district (Council of Urban Boards 1997, 29). This revocation had the effect of starting a major legal battle to determine when a charter school may be constituted as a legal entity independent of its sponsor district.

The Johnson Elementary School did revert to traditional public school status, but the dispute may lead to renewed calls and even legislation to protect charter schools from high-level board politics by clarifying California's charter process and allowing entities other than a school district to grant charters. On the other hand, it could lead to legislation that calls for district approval. It also is raising issues concerning appeal processes and whether they should be implemented and designed to appeal revocation by a district when the proponents disagree.

Educational Focus

The mission and philosophy of the O'Farrell Community School, a middle school in San Diego, are explained at the school's website. The mission statement came out of an August 1989 meeting at a planning retreat that included teachers, administrators, parents, and community groups. It states: "O'Farrell Community School: Center for Advanced Academic Studies will promote excellence by providing all middle school students a single, academically enriched curriculum within a multiethnic, student-centered environment. The mission of the school is to attend to the social, intellectual, psychological and physical needs of middle level youth so they will become responsible, literate, thinking and contributing citizens" (O'Farrell Community School website, 1).

The O'Farrell school commits itself to helping students engage in experiences that extend beyond the school site and to allowing students to see the social commitment involved in education. The school also helps students assess and evaluate their own performance by establishing significant goals with the students. The school seeks to make connections for students by having them work cooperatively in teams so they actively participate in their learning by exploring and analyzing concepts and ideas from various areas of study. The school also advocates applied learning in cross-curricular studies by helping students identify and solve academic problems in an interdisciplinary setting (O'Farrell Community School website, 1).

The O'Farrell Community School is a leader in the educational reform movement, and it is active in the National Alliance for Restructuring Education, a progressive educational nonprofit organization, and in the Coalition of Essential Schools.

Organizational Management and Educational Accountability

Some of the legal and political issues the school faces are no different from those of charter schools in numerous states. The school has a chief educational officer (CEO) and is established on the principles of teacher-community involvement, interagency collaboration, and interdisciplinary teaching (Council of Urban Boards 1997, 30). There have been controversies regarding staffing, funding and use of funds, and state accrediting laws, and the O'Farrell school had difficulty getting the state waivers it was promised under California law. Some of these problems have been resolved through mediation, but others continue to plague school operations.

The school has not severed ties with the district and relies on the district for some of the school's services. Some of its teachers retain their membership in the local teachers' union, and the National Education Association has worked closely with the school to ensure its success.

O'Farrell's 1,400 students are broken up into educational "families" of approximately 150 students each with six teachers per family. Each family receives the same curriculum. Three of the families serve the sixth-grade students, and six families serve the seventh- and eighth-grade students. Each educational family has a teacher designated as a family leader, and this teacher is responsible for the day-to-day operation of the family. Students attend class with teachers in their educational family all day except for a fifty-minute discovery class ((O'Farrell Community School website, 1).

The CEO is responsible for keeping the school functioning along the school's philosophical lines and has been called "the keeper of the dream." Teachers and classified personnel assume roles in the planning and operation of the school program. Leadership roles, as well as administrative duties, are shared by the teaching staff. Traditional vice-principal and head counselor positions were eliminated, and their district allocation was "cashed in" to pay teachers who take on additional leadership responsibilities. School-wide decisions are made by the Community Council, which is made up of team leaders, the CEO, a classified staff member, the magnet resource teacher, the administrative aide, a student and parent representative, the family advocate, and a media-technology representative (O'Farrell Community School website, 2).

In terms of evaluation and accountability, the charter of the O'-Farrell Community School states that 80 percent of the children who stay in school for three years will be able to enter any high school at the college preparatory level. O'Farrell students were slightly below district averages in reading, language arts, and mathematics as of this writing, but the school's teachers, maintaining that the district's standardized tests were not aligned with either the school's or the district's curriculum, said they believed a better indicator of the students' success and academic performance would be the students' high school performance. In the fall of 1996, an independent evaluator from the San Diego schools assessed how well 131 O'Farrell students in the class that had started at O'Farrell in 1992–1993 were faring at Morse High School. The analysis revealed the following:

> The O'Farrell students were enrolled and involved in more rigorous and advanced courses than other students in similar grades.
> The O'Farrell students were performing at higher levels in the courses studied as demonstrated by letter-grade distributions.
> In a standardized test given during the 1995–1996 school year, 53.6 percent of the O'Farrell students scored at or above the publisher's median in reading comprehension compared to 43.0 percent of their peers. Similarly, in mathematics, 66.3 percent of the O'Farrell students scored at or above the publisher's median compared to 56.3 percent of their peers.

The study also indicated that although the O'Farrell students might not be showing an immediate, consistent, or dramatic improvement in test scores, there appeared to be substantial progress. Furthermore, the school had the fifth-lowest suspension rate of the twenty-two middle schools and an average daily attendance rate of 96 percent (O'-Farrell Community School website, 2). These findings, in addition to vindicating the school and its students and teachers, were strong evidence regarding the inadequacy of relying solely on standardized testing.

To meet the social and economic needs of students and their parents, the school also has five social workers, three welfare eligibility workers, staff from twenty-five social service agencies on the premises, and a thrift shop (O'Farrell Community School website, 2). The educational views of the school can be found in the six major challenge areas developed within the curriculum:

1. Community service—Students are required to complete twelve hours of community service per year. Much like service learn-

ing, the requirement is designed to enhance altruism and citizenship skills among students.

2. Exhibition—Students at the school are required to present an exhibition during the fourth quarter of each year. The exhibition is designed to help students develop the art of self-assessment as they demonstrate and document their strengths and weaknesses.

3. Research process—Students are required to show that they can apply knowledge to real-life problems. They do this through research in various areas that requires them to gather information, use the information to describe and solve problems, and sustain an effort over time to complete important tasks.

4. O'Farrell presentation—To help students develop a better understanding of the school procedures, students are required to prepare a presentation for third persons not yet familiar with the school. The students must present the school's philosophy and procedures.

5. Academic performance—Students must meet the state guidelines and standards for education while at the same time benefit from performance and portfolio examinations.

6. The O'Farrell way—Students learn how to resolve conflicts, identify and solve problems, communicate and work collaboratively with others, and behave civilly. (O'Farrell Community School website)

Mater Center Charter School

Located in Hialeah, Florida, the Mater Center Charter School, which serves elementary school students, entered into contractual relationships with the sponsor, the School Board of Miami–Dade County, on 13 May 1998. The school seeks to establish an innovative program and has identified three basic concepts that it wishes to embrace. One, the school is devoted to the idea of a multi-age learning environment that allows children to learn and progress at their own pace. Two, the Mater Center Charter School is committed to small classroom sizes. Three, the school has a parental involvement obligation that is designed to ensure, wherever possible, that parents will actively participate in their child's education. The school sees its mission as providing a loving, caring, and supportive environment that encourages a love for learning (Mater Center Charter School 13 May 1998).

Total enrollment at the school was designed to be seventy-five, and in the first year, 1998–1999, the school offered education from kindergarten to fifth-grade students. This is expected to remain the student body size through 2001 (Mater Center Charter School 13 May 1998, 11).

The school's educational focus centers around teaching students to think abstractly and to develop as lifelong learners. The educational model of the Mater Center Charter School is also based on the theories and principles of Theodore Sizer's Coalition of Essential Schools. An abstract thinking curriculum is offered at all grade levels, and avenues of creativity are incorporated into the curriculum throughout. Learning is based on the philosophy that less is more. There is an integrated curriculum and guided research. The school believes that the intellectual focus of learning should be to engage young minds, encourage questioning, and alternative teaching strategies. At the Mater school, learning is personalized, and the staff is a participatory staff devoted to developing curriculum and changing teaching practices (Mater Center Charter School 2 February/5 March 1998, 10).

Educational Focus

The Mater Center Charter School's educational program is designed "to improve the academic performance of all students, including at-risk students, by tailoring the curriculum to the individual learning styles, by focusing on strengths, by setting high academic expectations, by viewing differences as assets rather than liabilities, and by incorporating best educational practices into classroom and curriculum" (Mater Center Charter School 2 February/5 March 1998, 13).

Developing a concept-based curriculum, the Mater Center Charter School seeks to frame learning tasks as complex problems, provide contexts that give meaning to facts, take informal knowledge seriously, allow for multiple right answers, and require long-term projects that promote socially constructed knowledge. To accomplish its educational focus, the school uses distinctive instructional methods such as whole language (whereby children learn to read in context and critically), thematic units, and cooperative learning. The school also maintains a code of conduct and management strategies to enhance the learning environment.

Organizational Management and Educational Accountability

Accountability is an important aspect of the school's philosophy. Cooperation and helpful feedback from all stakeholders are encouraged at the school to assess and help develop a learning environment. Methods for the assessment of student performance include facilitator observation, peer and self-evaluations, projects, presentations, exhibitions, and portfolios. The Stanford Achievement Test serves as the indicator for both the pre-planning phase and the reevaluation phase. The test is given in the beginning of the school year and is used as a baseline measurement for that year. Grade evaluations are conducted under the rubric of the Metropolitan Test, a state test, and key evaluations determine how well students are meeting their educational goals and standards.

The government and management of the school are carried out under the direction of the Board of Directors of Mater Center School Incorporated, a nonprofit Florida corporation. Although the board of directors has the final word as to the administration and accountability of the school, the administrative structure of the school consists of a head teacher who is responsible for the supervision of other teachers. He or she addresses student-related issues, assists in curriculum development, oversees parental involvement and contractual agreements, writes grants, and helps organize fund-raising events.

Teachers and teaching are held to standards adopted by the school, and teachers who are hired display an understanding of alternative approaches to curriculum development and presentation. The school reserves the right to fire teachers "at will" as long as no state or federal laws are violated. Teachers are hired for a ninety-day provisional time period, and their performance is then reviewed before full-time employment is offered.

The Mater Center Charter School promises to offer an exciting hands-on, personalized, and cooperative approach to learning that is both engaging and cognitively demanding. Developing a curriculum based on multi-age learning and interdisciplinary approaches to learning makes this charter school another unique experiment within the charter movement.

Pimeria Alta School

Pimeria Alta School is a high school located in Nogales, Arizona, two blocks from the border with Mexico. The school was established in June 1995 by the superintendent of schools for Santa Cruz County, Robert Canchola, and a former innovative and experienced Arizona teacher, Sandra Potter. This was one year after Arizona passed the state's charter legislation. The school opened with 13 students, in 1999 served 248 students, and is expected to open its second campus in Santa Cruz County sometime in the year 2000. It serves students from fourteen to twenty-two in grades seven through twelve.

According to its mission statement, the goal of Pimeria Alta

School is "to provide opportunities for historically disenfranchised students to obtain a valid high school diploma through flexible, innovative and creative means, and to provide students and community members with options for transition into various lifestyles which would further their efforts to continue as lifelong students" (Pimeria Alta School 1996).

Frustrated by a lack of schools in the surrounding area that serviced disenfranchised adolescents, especially Hispanic youth, both Canchola and Potter saw charter legislation as an opportunity to create an educational environment that would provide an alternative to what they saw as a public school system that was failing the local youth. They wanted to provide a safe and positive learning environment for students that would engage them and show them the importance and relevancy of education. A huge percentage of the young people in Santa Cruz County were idle and not attending any school, either having been expelled or having simply dropped out of education altogether. These young people saw no relevance in their educational experience, and, in fact, their past experience in the traditional public schools had left them marginalized, bored with schooling, and unable to connect to academic pursuits.

When the school first opened in October 1995, 60 percent of the students were adjudicated by the criminal court system. Only seven of the students were female, because the school was looked at as a school for "bad boys" and the community was leery of sending its girls to be a part of such a student body. This situation, however, has changed. By March 2000, only 6 percent of the students in attendance are adjudicated through the court system, and 52 percent of the student body is female (March 2000 interview with Sandra Potter). As of March 2000, the school had become the third-largest high school in the county of Santa Cruz, Arizona.

Pimeria Alta School began with a staff of seven people, of which only two were teachers. At its campus in Nogales, in March 2000 there are twenty-two staff members, seven teachers, and two teacher interns who are working toward certification. The ratio of students to teachers is eleven to one, and the school prides itself on providing individualized instruction based on specific student needs along with dynamic group instruction. Each student has an independent educational program, which is used to map out or chart the student's needs.

In 1995 when the school first opened, Pimeria Alta received $30,000 in federal funds, and when Canchola established the school as a new school district, the school could then also receive immediate state funds. The city of Nogales initially permitted the school to share facilities with the local community college, which allowed the school to avoid the costly start-up costs that are often associated with charter schools. As of March 2000, the school receives $1.2 million in state funds per year as well as $350,000 from the federal government. In addition, the school receives money from tobacco grants, school-to-work grants, and private grants.

Educational Focus

The school's site in Nogales is a storefront school located in a shopping mall. The windows are stained glass, having been made by the students, and the inside of the school is elaborately decorated with student work in the form of murals, pottery, stained glass, and other art forms.

The curriculum for the school is a humanistic core curriculum based on academic necessities for admission to colleges and universities. It is an integrated, project-centered curriculum, and much of the core-curriculum instruction relies on the use of computers. The instructional program for the school's core curriculum is fueled by NovaNet, an online computer process, and the writing and literature components are integrated separately into the school curriculum. When the school first opened, students had the use of two computers; there are now fifty-eight computers in the school.

In 1997, the school adopted the school-to-work concept. A health occupation program was established that provides for state certification for nursing assistants and physical therapist aides. The program is community based, which means that community members may also attend. The program has been highly successful, graduating many health professionals.

Besides the core curriculum and the health occupation program, the school has complemented its program in various unique ways by adopting some innovative approaches to education. Pimeria Alta has a tolerance program that is offered to all students. This program is the result of the educational philosophy of the school and one of its founders, Sandra Potter, that encourages an appreciation of diversity and antiracist, antisexist education. The school also has a stained-glass program and a pottery program, both of which allow students kinesthetic learning and creative expression. The school also has a music studio where students can learn to mix music, make compact discs, and learn studio composition. There are also internships offered by the local radio and television stations.

Teachers work collectively, and on the third Friday of every month they are given planning time, either jointly or separately, so they might prepare for high-quality instruction. Although Arizona does not mandate that teachers need to be certified, both Canchola and Potter require that Pimeria Alta hire only certified teachers in order to assure quality instruction. Teachers are constantly encouraged to increase their professional development through paid attendance at educational conferences and continuing education.

Organizational Management and Educational Accountability

The Pimeria Alta School became nonprofit in 1998, and three board members make decisions for the school with the help of students and parents. There is an on-site advisory council made up of the chief educational officer, two community members, two parents, one student, one certified staff member, and one noncertified staff member. The on-site advisory council offers recommendations and suggestions to the board, which uses them to make decisions and solve problems. The idea was that the school would be a community-based school, meaning that the community would take over the management of the school from the nonprofit board in ten years. This change is still envisioned, and the school is preparing for the eventual community takeover.

Students are evaluated according to standards adopted by the state of Arizona. The Pimeria Alta charter is a fifteen-year charter that is reviewed every five years based on performance relative to the state standards. The charter is reviewed and evaluated by the State Board for Charter Schools, a separate and distinct public entity from the Arizona State Board of Education. Working with students, the staff makes sure that they understand what is expected of them and helps them meet specific target goals. Since its inception in 1995, the school has graduated 168 high school students, and 36 students have completed the health occupation program. The Pimeria Alta staff tracks the progress of students once they have left the school, and as of spring 2000, 27 percent of the graduates were pursuing higher educational goals.

Although the community of Nogales was tentative about the idea of such a school, it has now embraced Pimeria Alta as an example of one of its most successful endeavors. Because of the nature of the community—many of the parents are poor and working class—parental involvement is not what it might be, but even so, parental support is overwhelming. All and all, the school is considered a tremendous success, which has encouraged the founders and the board to expand services by opening a second campus in the Green Valley area of Santa Cruz County in the year 2000.

CONCLUSION

Thousands of charter schools across the country are designing and pursuing diverse curriculums and educational approaches to learning. As this book is being written, charter schools springing up throughout the United States plan to offer varied educational roads to student learning. How these schools will fare and how they will affect the future of public education will be the subject of much debate and inquiry as the charter idea begins to take a firm hold in communities throughout the country.

REFERENCES

Alianza School website: www.alianza.santacruz.k12.ca.us

Charter School of San Diego website: www.charterschool-sandiego.net

Freire Charter School website: www.libertynet.org/freire

Greene, D. "Elaine C. Young: A Quest for a School Designed by Children." *Westchester Weekly Desk,* 28 February 1999.

Mater Center Charter School. "Contract." Hialeah, FL, 13 May 1998.

———. "Proposal." Hialeah, FL, submitted 2 February 1998, revised 5 March 1998.

Miner, B. "Bilingual Education: New Visions for a New Era." *Rethinking Schools* 13, no. 4 (Summer 1999): 1, 18–20.

Minnesota New Country School website: http://mncs.K12.mn.us

Nathan, Joe. *Charter Schools: Creating Hope and Opportunity for American Education.* San Francisco: Jossey-Bass, 1996.

O'Farrell Community School website: http://edweb.sdsu.edu./O'Farrell/O'Farrellhome.html

Pimeria Alta School. "Mission Statement," 1997.

Rethinking Schools 10, no. 3 (Spring 1996): 10.

Saks, Judith B. *The Basics of Charter Schools: A School Board Primer.* Alexandria, VA: National School Boards Association, 1997.

Wallis, Claudia. "A Class of Their Own." *Time,* 31 October 1994.

Chapter Four

~ Charter Schools and the Law

For many charter school advocates, charter schools are not so much about individual schools as they are about reforming districts and school systems. In fact, many people would argue that charter schools are all about trying to change the system of education in the United States by allowing for public choice within public schools. By the year 2000, the growth of the charter school idea was dramatic, and that growth has meant the development, debate, implementation, and monitoring of new state laws. Any discussion of legal issues regarding charters must be undertaken with the understanding that the charter movement is a "living mosaic"—one that is susceptible to change at any given moment.

There is no national or federal charter school policy, and because charter school legislation varies so dramatically from state to state, each state in which a charter school is proposed must be examined separately (Hassel 1995). For example, in New Hampshire, local boards are the approving agencies and sponsors, and state boards operate for appeal purposes. New Jersey approves charters through a state commissioner, and in Florida, the approving agencies are local boards and universities and colleges. New Mexico approves charters through state boards, and Arizona has a state board for charter approval.

If a charter is denied by the approving agency, many states have an appeal process, but many do not. Arkansas approves or denies a charter school through its state board along with local board and bargaining unit approval. There is no appeal process. California approves charters through local boards and does have an appeal process for denial that is handled by a county panel (Council of Urban Boards of Education 1997).

Many states "cap" the number of charters that are allowed in a state and can also cap them by districts. Alaska caps the state level at thirty while permitting one to ten charter schools per district. Wisconsin has no caps on the number of charter schools that can be developed and operated. Issues regarding waivers of most state education laws and regulations vary from state to state as well. Although Rhode Island forces charter schools to apply for waivers, North Carolina waives state laws and regulations automatically.

Many state charter school laws grant local school boards a great deal of say concerning the creation of charter schools in their jurisdictions. In 1998, only twenty-one of the thirty-five charter school laws empowered any entity to grant charters without the agreement of the local school board (Kolderie 1995, 148). Although many pundits and charter school devotees argue that this restriction hinders the creation and operation of charter schools, boards argue that without the ability to monitor and control charter schools, the charter school experiment would essentially be unregulated, which could mean unwanted fiscal and political consequences and implications. Tension concerning theories of regulation is characteristic of the charter movement.

When addressing issues of employment and collective bargaining with classified and certified staff, some states allow their charter schools to bargain independently and directly with staff while others do not. Minnesota, for example, allows independent and direct bargaining between the charter schools and their employees and staff while Kansas does not.

Similarly, many states allow the charter schools to operate as independent legal entities while some states do not. In Georgia, charter schools may be independent legal entities, but they cannot be in Rhode Island. Many states, such as Wyoming, have not specified whether charter schools can be legal entities in and of themselves.

Only twenty of the thirty-five charter laws on the books at the end of 1998 allowed charter schools to exist as separate legal entities. In the other fifteen states and districts, charter schools had no independent status; like conventional public schools, they were to be treated as divisions or branches of their local school districts. And of the twenty states that did allow legal independence from the governing school board, that independence was not required. In California's initial 1992 charter law for example, a charter's legal status was to be determined by an agreement negotiated by the school and the district (Kolderie 1995, 148). Amendments to California charter school laws in 1998 made it clear that charter schools could be incorporated as independent nonprofit institutions. In Colorado, charter schools are units of local school districts with no independent legal status, yet they operate with relative freedom with regard to the essential operational elements of their schools.

How charter schools are chartered, that is, the legal status and independence given to them, has a great deal of effect on the day-to-day operations of each charter school. Many pundits and educational reformers argue that charter schools must have the autonomy to innovate and act independent of their school districts and state legislatures if the charter school experiment is to be authentically implemented and studied. Each state must consider the complexity of its own particular educational and political environments and then design charter laws that meet the needs of the citizens and communities.

That is the subject of political debate in all states and the reason for the disparity in legal status and operation of charter schools among states. For example, in Colorado, the Denver School Board is challenging the constitutionality of the charter law, questioning whether the state legislature had the legal right to grant the state agency the power to grant charters in the first place (Council of Urban Boards of Education 1997, 40–41). In Denver, the school board once again turned down the Thurgood Marshall school, a charter school whose application had been turned down twice before, stating that Colorado's constitution gives local school boards specific authority for instruction. The state board's ability to tell a local school board that it must approve a charter offering a certain kind of instruction, the Denver board argues, is clearly an incursion into legal local authority.

Citizens in some states draft referendums and state statutes that would constrain a local school board's discretion so that a charter must be granted to any group that can meet established criteria. These citizens advocate the development of what they term "objective standards and criteria" that would be used to protect qualified charter advocates from school boards that seek to restrain the development of charters.

Although the charter school idea is still in its infancy, a number of charter schools have closed or have had their charters legally revoked because of financial problems or mismanagement. In Arizona, a state grand jury indicted the founder of Citizen 2000, a bankrupt Phoenix charter school, on thirty-one counts of theft, fraud, and the misuse of $179,000 in public money (Council of Urban Boards of Education 1997, 41). And in Washington, D.C., the Marcus Garvey Charter School became the center of a controversy involving the alleged mistreatment of a news reporter and possible theft of property. The issue there revolved around the closeness of supervision between the charter operator and the board of education that approved the charter (Nelson 1997).

These and other unforeseen crises with regard to certain charter schools make it clear how important the local school board's oversight role can be. They also point to the need for continued regulation and monitoring of charter schools as their operation has been found to be both beneficial and difficult. Reviewing, monitoring, and otherwise overseeing a charter school can be hard work. For charter schools to become a central part of the educational picture, they must have clear and reliable relationships with the community agencies that can authorize the charters and guarantee funding, develop effective communication channels, and hold school operators accountable to their promises.

Another aspect of charter school laws and their legal status is the scope of exemptions from state laws and regulations such schools receive. Charter school advocates argue that in order to be truly effective, charter schools must receive automatic exemptions from state laws and regulations (with the exception of provisions regarding health, safety, nondiscrimination, nonreligiosity, and other core public school laws). Exemption from what charter advocates deem bureaucratic regulations is a central demand of the charter movement.

STATE LAWS THAT AFFECT CHARTER SCHOOLS

Certain specific provisions of state laws impact the development and operation of charter schools. Some of these legal issues involve funding, district revenues, collective bargaining issues, admission policies, autonomy, equity, and accountability.

Funding and the Law

The primary source of revenues for charter schools is the public coffer. Although state funding formulas vary, they all attempt to provide a fair share of public funds for each student who wishes to attend a charter school. Because the needs of the students vary widely, from special education needs to socioeconomic ones, funding can be a complicated issue. And because charter school funding comes from public districts, as we shall see when we turn our eye to the politics of charter schools, revenues and funding are two of the chief political issues facing the charter movement. Before looking at funding issues, it might be best to look first at charter school costs.

Charter School Costs

The costs associated with charter schools can be separated into start-up costs and ongoing expenses. For new charter schools, start-up costs can be quite high—especially during the initial year—and charter schools that convert existing public or private schools to charter schools must bear the cost of conversion; by far the most significant cost is the cost of the facility. Building codes, insurance concerns, and local regulations often require renovation of existing buildings for charter school use. The cost of readying a facility for use as a charter school and assuring that construction complies with local regulations can be both costly and bureaucratic. Staffing can be an expensive cost as well. The staff must have orientation and be prepared for the opening of the school. Schools also need equipment and resources, and these costs must be funded initially by the school through private or nonprofit sources. Accounting systems, security systems, and the like all work together to create significant costs, especially initially.

Once the schools are open, the ongoing expenses begin to resemble those of a regular public school. The only difference between the two is the charter school's ability to control and maintain its own budget and financial identity in accordance with its specific needs. Salaries and benefits make up the lion's share of the ongoing costs, but the day-to-day operation of the school must also be factored into ongoing costs.

Because charter schools control their own budgets, their spending is not monitored or handled by the local school district through the central office. Charter schools have the flexibility to spend their money any way their governing bodies see fit. Their autonomy provides them more flexibility and freedom than the conventional schools have. For example, charter schools can usually design salary schedules and systems of compensation to meet their particular needs.

Charter School Funding

Funding is the critical issue for charter schools, and it affects them in a myriad of ways. States set their own formulas and establish their own funding mechanisms, and the mechanisms differ from state to state. For example, some states, such as Michigan, Massachusetts, and Hawaii, have established clear funding levels in their charter school legislation. In other states, such as Colorado, the funding levels are set on a school-by-school basis. Colorado funding levels start at 80 percent of the district per-pupil operating costs and then go up based on negotiations. Revenues that go to charter schools reduce a district's overall available funds, which has led to a source of tension and debate among school boards, parents, legislators, and governors. In fact, it is one of the major points of contention between advocates of charter school proposals and people who are opposed to the charter idea.

The American Federation of Teachers (AFT) has argued that charter schools impose new costs on districts and that they are not necessarily underfunded when all public revenue sources are matched to the specific kinds of students educated in charter schools. In fact, the AFT argues, unless a charter school primarily serves at-risk children, it is probably overfunded. The AFT also found that charter schools add new fixed costs, new facility costs, new start-up costs, new costs associated with private school to charter school enrollment shifts, and, in fact, are not underfunded, as charter school advocates claim, but receive excess funding (Nelson 1997, 1).

One of the biggest problems for Minnesota charter schools is financing. In order to reduce class size and implement other reforms, these schools relied on asking experienced teachers to accept low salaries and take on administrative and other responsibilities at no cost. Basic equipment and facility financing were also problems for many charter schools in Minnesota, and private sources had to be sought to continue long-term support (Molnar 1996, 4). As a result, many of the teachers at charter schools find they do more for less salary.

Financing problems are not unique to Minnesota but seem to be universal around the country. In a University of Minnesota study of charter schools throughout the United States, the authors found that financial support and a lack of start-up funds were the most frequently mentioned problems charter schools face (University of Minnesota Humphrey Institute 1996). The new costs associated with charter schools have not been adequately addressed in many if not most states.

Current levels of per-pupil funding may not meet the need of many charter schools (Hassel 1999, 106). First, the start-up costs associated with charter schools for the first year of operation generally must be funded separately because the schools do not receive public funds until the fall. Second, many charters must pay the cost of their facilities separately from the operating costs, which are covered by the per-pupil funds. As a result, many charter schools must scramble to obtain funds from sources other than public revenues. And this situation, argue those people who are less than enamored with the charter school idea, allows private companies to influence the governing and curriculum at many charter schools because the companies offer prepackaged managerial solutions to public financial problems. For example, the AFT found in a study of six states and their funding levels that

- Arizona charters receive overfunding in the amount of $1,000 per pupil
- Minnesota's charter school overfunding is about $200 per pupil for elementary students and $1,000 per pupil for high school students
- Colorado's charter school overfunding is $1,200 per pupil
- California's charter school overfunding is about $500 per pupil
- Massachusetts' charter school overfunding is so large it was not measurable
- Michigan's charter school overfunding is about $600. (Nelson 1997, 5)

District Revenues and the Law

In a September 1996 article in *Phi Delta Kappan,* Eric Premack, director of the Charter Schools Project and Development Center of the Institute for Education Reform at California State University at Sacramento, noted that the fiscal effect of a charter school on a district depends on the nature of the district and its legal charter. Premack found that "districts in a declining enrollment mode often find that revenues drop faster than expenditures due to the fixed costs. The bite can be particularly severe if the district is left with a disproportionately higher level of senior and higher paid teachers" (Premack 1996, 14). According to Premack, some districts levy an oversight or overhead charge on the charter school, which is much like a surcharge paid initially for the cost of doing business.

Teacher Issues and the Law

Many of the state laws are unclear about collective bargaining, retirement benefits, and other issues that affect both teachers and school boards. In fifteen states and the District of Columbia, charter schools may act as their own employers, but in the remaining ten states, teachers must be employees of the local district. In thirteen states, charter schools are subject to state collective bargaining laws, but in six others, the legislation does not address collective bargaining arrangements. The remaining states and the District of Columbia either exclude charter schools from collective bargaining arrangements or allow schools to address collective bargaining as part of their charters (Council of Urban Boards of Education 1997). Many of the above issues are being negotiated, and this picture of charter schools is constantly changing.

Concerning the issue of teacher retirement, some states stipulate that teachers either must participate in or be eligible for the state retirement system, but as to the issue of who pays for that participation, many state laws remain silent. If charter school teachers continue to be school district employees, the district may share in the cost of the retirement benefits. But if the charter school is the employer, that school may have to use its own funds to contribute to the retirement system.

As one example of state law in this area, Minnesota allows teachers to continue to accrue district retirement credits while at a charter school, but they must pay both employer and employee contributions. In Florida, a charter school may be either a public or a private employer. As a public employer, the charter school may choose to participate in the state's retirement system; if it does, then employees become compulsory members of that system.

Other states, like Colorado and Minnesota, provide protected leaves of absence so teachers can leave their public school posts and teach in charter schools. Other states, however, like Georgia and New Mexico, do not even include or mention a leave for teachers in their state laws.

Admission Policies and the Law

Some states require that charter schools admit students through a lottery system while others require schools to give preference to those students who live in geographic proximity to the school. In a few states, the law allows charter schools to limit admission based on the subject area focus of the school.

Autonomy and the Law

Autonomy is a critical issue in determining the rights and responsibilities of charter schools—how they operate and how they govern. The degree of charter school autonomy can influence the way charter schools and local districts interact and thus can be indicative of success or failure. The states with stronger charter legislation grant a broad autonomy by waiving state regulation requirements, offering a number of sponsorship options, and providing an appeal process when an applicant for a charter is denied. Some states see fit to grant what they call a "super-waiver," which sweeps away volumes of legal and regulatory red tape. In states that do not have such detailed legislation, the charter schools must legally remain part of a school district and may be afforded no greater autonomy than a traditional public school.

Equity and the Law

Probably one of the most controversial and closely observed areas of charter school law concerns the educational impact of charter schools on issues of equity. Many state laws do not address the issue of racial imbalance or balance in charter schools, presumably expecting them to abide by state and federal laws. Some states, however, explicitly state that charter schools must not violate state or federal nondiscrimination laws. Other states, like Michigan, mandate that the charter schools in their states operate in accordance with court orders involving racial desegregation. Some states require that charter schools reflect the racial composition of the area in which the school is located.

A major "desegregation case" could be pending because different states embrace different approaches to charter schools. Many activists in the area of civil rights and desegregation are very concerned about the impact of charter schools on educational equity and racial segregation and are monitoring the success and failure of various state charter schools in this regard.

Accountability and the Law

Charter school advocates would like to frame the issue of accountability as one of choice. Real accountability, they argue, is imposed by competition in the marketplace, and charter schools provide this competition. Parents who know what is best for their children and are empowered to choose schools will send their children to schools that actually function, argue many charter school proponents. Although this reasoning has a resounding populist appeal, the decision where to send one's child to school is far more complex than simply basing the decision on academic excellence and choice. Proximity to the school and work, transportation, work schedules, availability of child care, and the type of extracurricular activities that are available also have a bearing on where parents send their children to school (Molnar 1996, 4). For many charter school advocates and critics, the social and economic issues that face parents, students, and teachers cannot be separated from the issue of choice, who gets it, and how it is framed.

And what happens when a charter school fails? This is the ultimate question for states as charter schools are supposed to introduce accountability throughout local school districts as well as within a specific charter school. Even though this question should be a priority for states interested in charter school legislation, charter school evangelists such as Chester Finn, Bruno Manno, and Louann Bierlein, the authors of *Charter Schools in Action: What Have We Learned?* (1997), have not found a single state with a well-formed plan for dealing with contingencies of failure and accountability such as malfeasance, corruption, abuse, and immorality among charter schools (Finn, Manno, and Bierlein 1997).

In principle, each charter school signs a contract with its charter-granting agency that spells out the academic results the school is expected to achieve throughout the term of the charter. And, of course, each school must meet state academic standards. For example, a school might promise that a certain proportion of its students will perform above grade average or level on a particular assessment over a specific period of time. When it comes time to reconsider the granting or the renewal of the charter, the charter-granting agency can evaluate the school's progress relative to specifically spelled out and articulated standards as well as its performance in meeting state standards. The school can then have its charter regranted based on its performance or denied because of nonconformity with prearticulated and state-mandated goals. Because of the newness of the charter school movement, however, the Hudson Institute's nationwide study of charter schools concluded that "today's charter school accountability systems remain underdeveloped, often clumsy and ill-fitting, and are themselves beset by dilemmas" (Manno et al. 1997, 1).

Charter-granting agencies in various states are still struggling with how charter schools should fit into the existing structure of legal standards and testing processes. Questions as to what to precisely implement to achieve charter school goals and accountability, how to handle accountability, and what actions to take before a school's charter renewal date are all being debated. Until charter-granting agencies have clear processes in place with detailed policy statements and missions, taxpayers and parents cannot feel confident that charter schools will be held to accountability standards. From the perspective of the charter schools themselves, a lack of clearly stated accountability procedures is threatening because there are no specific accountability systems the charter schools can rely on. Holding charter schools accountable for results is one of the big issues facing those schools and the states that license and charter them.

LEGAL ACCOUNTABILITY OF CHARTER SCHOOLS

Even though charter schools are often exempt from many state and local laws through the use of legal waivers, they are still subject to some restrictions. First and foremost, charter schools remain subject to federal laws, which states cannot waive. The schools must provide free and appropriate education to children with special needs, respect students' constitutional rights, maintain nondiscriminatory policies in admissions and other areas, and refrain from teaching religion. Second, most state charter school laws leave at least some state-level school laws in place for charter schools. For example, some charter school laws require that each charter school submit an annual report of its activities (Hassel 1995, 161). Charter schools must also fulfill a host of state reporting requirements to assure compliance with state charter laws and other federal and state laws.

UNDERSTANDING CHARTER SCHOOL LAWS IN ONE STATE: MICHIGAN

How different states deal with the promulgation and passage of various charter school laws varies with the politics of each state. Each state must deal with political forces and state constitutional laws that define the scope of the charter laws the state agencies adopt. Although the situation may vary from state to state, the struggle for charter school laws and their acceptance defines the legislation and, thus, the types of charter schools and governance that each state will recognize.

In 1993, for example, political forces in Michigan converged to produce a remarkable result: the elimination of property taxes as a source of school funding. This action meant that school districts would be in dire straits financially. Although Michigan was relatively prosperous, most of the prosperity was in the cities and their suburbs. In addition, the state had done little to equalize spending among school districts. In 1991–1992, state equalization funds provided just 48.5 percent of the average school spending, making Michigan one of only fourteen states in which this percentage fell below 50 percent (Vergari 1995).

With the passage of the 1993 tax law, the state's political leaders instigated a political and fiscal crisis within the state's schools. Facing a $6.7-billion shortfall in the budget for education, it was vitally urgent that the state's policymakers engage in sensible educational planning. With a constitutional amendment needed to increase sales taxes—the alternative to property taxes proposed by legislators—the policymakers needed to act quickly. In addition to the fiscal crisis facing the Michigan schools, there was a nonprofit community movement called TEACH Michigan. This movement hoped to institute a system of vouchers that would allow families to spend tax dollars to send their children to private or parochial schools. Although Michigan's constitution prohibits such programs of privatization, the director of TEACH Michigan, Paul DeWeese, was busy mobilizing support for a referendum to amend that constitutional provision (Christoff 16 September 1993).

In October 1993, Governor John Engler delivered an address to the state legislature outlining his proposals for educational reform (Engler 1993; Christoff 5 October 1993). He proposed a package that included:

- Major changes to the state's tax code
- An overhaul of school finance centered on a state-funded foundation grant program that would ensure that all districts had adequate resources
- Gubernatorial appointment of a state school superintendent
- A study of school district consolidation
- Major changes in school labor laws, including abolishing tenure and granting teachers the right not to join a union
- A state-mandated core curriculum and a statewide system of "report cards" to measure and ensure student progress

◆ Inter- and intradistrict public school choice. (Hassel 1999)

Engler also proposed a charter school program that was far more liberal in its operations than charter school programs in other states. For example, the range of organizations empowered to apply for and receive a charter (in addition to local school boards, intermediate school boards, and the state board of education) included university and community boards of trustees, a newly created state charter school authority, and any public body other than a charter school. In fact, a "public body" was defined by Michigan to mean:

> A state officer, agency, department, division, bureau, board, commission, council, authority or other body in the executive, judicial or legislative branch of the state government; a county, city, township, village, regional governing body, or council, special district, or municipal corporation, or a board, department, commission, council, or agency thereof; or any other body created by state or local government. (Michigan Senate Bill 896, 1993, as introduced, 2–3)

Also proposed were the legal independence of charter schools, automatic waivers of state laws, no cap on the number of charter schools in the state, and full per-pupil funding.

The Republican legislators, encouraged by the political climate in the state and influenced by the fiscal crisis inherent in the school budgets, introduced two separate but identical bills. House Bill 5124 was introduced by Representative William Bryant, and Senate Bill 896 was introduced by Senator Richard Posthumous (Nathan 1996, 167-205). The Senate bill, as approved by the Senate Education Committee, passed on 2 November 1993. Michigan's new charter law contained fewer compromises than the laws of other states; it enabled a wide range of groups to apply for charter status; it allowed applicants to approach a variety of potential authorizers, not just the boards of local school districts, but those of intermediate school districts, community colleges, and public universities as well; and it set no cap on the number of charter schools that could be chartered by the state. Finally, Michigan decreed that charter schools be subject to all state school laws.

Michigan's experience with charter school laws may be unique to that state, but the struggle and dialogue regarding charter school legislation in Michigan are being experienced by all states involved in the charter school experiment.

DIRECTIONS IN THE LAW

Some charter school proponents argue that the autonomy of charter schools is a critical issue and actually advocate that state laws should:

- Not set limits on the number of charters within a state or district
- Set few or no limits on who can apply for a charter
- Authorize a large number of entities to grant charters, such as education boards, colleges, universities, and local school boards
- Treat individual charter schools as if they were separate local educational authorities
- Provide financial and technical assistance in acquiring facilities for the schools and for start-up costs and state aid programs
- Specify that charter schools are qualified to receive federal, state, and even local revenues
- Waive a variety of state and local regulations that govern public schools
- Not require staff and teachers to meet state certification requirements that would apply in public schools
- Allow flexibility and room in the selection of accountability criteria to be used for renewal of the charter
- Assure that admission practices are not selective and that they promote racial diversity (Nathan 1996, 167–205, and Hassel 1999)

As we shall see, these legal issues are the subject of never-ending debate and controversy. What direction a state law takes has a great deal to do with the efficacy of charter schools. And although charter schools are released from burdensome regulations, they are still subject to federal and state constitutions as well as to federal and state discrimination laws. For example, the New Jersey State Supreme Court has decided to hear arguments by four school districts that claim the New Jersey charter school program is unconstitutional. Charter schools currently educate more than 10,000 students in New Jersey, and the school districts argue that the New Jersey charter legislation amounts to "taxation without representation" because the charter schools have no elected school boards ("Metro News Briefs" 1999). If the school districts prevail, the decision will have dramatic effects, not just on New Jersey, but on all states that have passed charter legislation.

LOOKING AT CHARTER LAWS STATE BY STATE

The following brief look at charter laws state by state is developed from the work of Joe Nathan in his book *Charter Schools: Creating Hope and Opportunity for American Education* (Nathan 1996, 167–205). Although the list includes all states as of the end of 1996, changes in state laws continue. For this reason, it is important for the reader to update and revise this list.

Alaska 1995

Adopted in 1995, Alaska's charter school legislation permits up to thirty charter schools. All charter schools in the state must be approved by both the local school board within which they operate and the state board of education. There is no appeal from a local board's denial of a charter. Charter schools in Alaska may not employ or bargain with staff independently, and the schools operate under a limited term with a performance-based contract. Alaska's legislation does not exempt charter schools from most state rules and regulations; charter initiators may apply for a waiver of local policies only. As of the 1999–2000 school year, Alaska had opened eighteen charter schools (Center for Education Reform website).

Arizona 1994

Arizona's charter law, passed in 1994, permits three different organizations to sponsor charter schools within the state: local districts, the state board of education, and any new state-chartering agency may charter a school. There is no appeal process from the denial of a charter; however, the initiator may apply to multiple grantors. There are no caps on the number of charter schools the state may charter. Charter schools receive an automatic waiver from most state education laws and regulations, and they may employ and/or bargain with staff independent of local bargaining units. Charter schools are independent legal entities in Arizona, and they receive a fifteen-year charter term. Arizona is considered to be a beacon for charter school experimentation and legislation, and approximately 348 charter schools were operating in Arizona during the 1997–1998 school year (Center for Education Reform website).

Arkansas 1995

According to a 1995 Arkansas law, only existing public schools may apply for charter status, and these schools must have the approval of both the school board that governs them and the state board of education. Any petition requesting a charter must also be approved by the local teachers' union, by at least two-thirds of the certified teachers at the school requesting the proposal, and by at least two-thirds of the parents present at a meeting called for the purpose of deciding whether to move ahead on the petition. There is no limit on the number of charter schools that can be started in the state, and the state board of education can waive rules and regulations. There is no appeal of a charter denial in Arkansas, nor is there any automatic waiver of state education laws and regulations, although waivers may be applied for and granted. Arkansas charter schools are not independent entities; they cannot bargain with or employ staff independently. All Arkansas charter schools operate under a long-term contract based on performance. As of December 1999, no charter schools had been opened in Arkansas (Center for Education Reform website).

California 1992

California legislation permitted up to 100 charters in 1992. The state board of education decided that it had the power to waive the law, and by 1998, there were 130 charter schools operating in the state. California has raised the number of charter schools that can be opened in California each year to 100. Charter schools must be approved by the local school board and by a county school district or by a county panel on appeal from a local district. Charter schools in California receive an automatic waiver from state education laws and regulations, and they are independent legal entities that can employ and/or bargain independently with their staffs. All charter schools are operated under a five-year, limited-term, performance-based contract. There are 234 open and operating charter schools operating in the state as of the 1999–2000 school year (Center for Education Reform website).

Colorado 1993

Anyone requesting charter status in Colorado must specify which state rules and regulations they wish to have waived. It is then up to the state board of education to determine which rules and regulations it will waive. Colorado legislation of 1993 requires that people who wish to start a charter school seek approval from the local school board. If the local board rejects the proposal, it can be appealed to the state board of education, which can approve or turn the appeal down. In 1999 Colorado had sixty-eight charter schools operating in the state (Center for Education Reform website).

Connecticut 1996

A 1996 Connecticut law permits up to twenty-four charter schools; of those schools, up to twelve must be authorized by local school boards and up to twelve may be authorized by the state board of education. Schools authorized by local school boards must conform to the local collective bargaining agreements. Charter denials may be appealed to the state board, which may order the local board to grant a charter. There is no automatic waiver of state education laws and regulations, but such waivers may be applied for. Charter schools are independent legal entities in the state of Connecticut, and they may employ and/or bargain with their staffs independently. They operate under a limited-term, performance-based contract. As of the 1999–2000 school year, Connecticut had seventeen charter schools (Center for Education Reform website).

Delaware 1995

In Delaware, 1995 legislation allows for the creation of an unlimited number of charter schools, but such schools must enroll students in at least two grades and have at least 200 students, except for charter schools serving at-risk or special need students, and even those schools must enroll at least 100 students. Charter schools may be approved by either a local school board or the state board of education. There is no appeal process for the denial of a charter. Charter schools in the state are automatically granted waivers from state education laws and regulations. Delaware charters are independent entities that can employ and negotiate directly and independently with their staffs. In 1999, five charter schools were open in the state (Center for Education Reform website).

District of Columbia 1996

The U.S. Congress authorized charter schools to operate in the District of Columbia in 1996. Charter schools must be approved by either the local school board or a special charter school authorizing committee. Appeals are subject to judicial review. There is an automatic waiver from state education laws and regulations. The charter schools in the District of Columbia are independent entities with the ability to employ and/or bargain with their staffs directly and independently. Charter schools operate under performance-based contracts of fifteen years. There are twenty-eight charter schools operating within the district (Center for Education Reform website).

Florida 1996

A 1996 Florida law allows for school districts and public state universities to sponsor charter schools. Although the legislation limits the number of charter schools that each district may sponsor, the law gives each district the right to appeal any charter denial to the state board of education. The state board of education forwards its recommendation to the local school board, and the local school board is asked to follow the state board's recommendation regarding the charter proposal. A local district that does not follow the state board's recommendation must explain its decision in writing. Florida charter schools receive an automatic waiver from state education laws and regulations, and they can negotiate directly with employees regarding salaries and hiring. Florida charter schools receive a term-based contract based on performance. In 1999, there were 112 charter schools operating in the state (Center for Education Reform website).

Georgia 1993

Georgia in 1993 initially permitted the conversion of existing public schools into charter schools, and the law was changed in 1998 to permit the creation of entirely new charter schools. The local school board in a particular town within which the charter school will operate must approve either a conversion or a new school. Charters that are denied cannot be appealed in Georgia. The schools can bargain directly with employees, but the charter schools are not independent entities and are subject to a term-based contract based on performance. As of the 1999–2000 school year, Georgia had thirty-two charter schools (Center for Education Reform website).

Hawaii 1994

The entire state of Hawaii is a single school district. An existing public school may ask for permission to operate as a "student-centered school," but before such a proposal is submitted, it must be approved by 60 percent of the school's administration, support staff, teaching personnel, and parents. According to 1994 legislation, charter schools are exempt from most school code regulations but must adhere to collective bargaining agreements, civil rights legislation, health and safety regulations, and performance standards. Hawaii has no appeal process for charters that are denied. Nor is it specified in state law if individual charter schools may employ and/or otherwise contract directly with staff. Hawaii charter schools are subject to a performance-based term contract. As of the 1999–2000 school year, Hawaii had two charter schools (Center for Education Reform website).

Idaho 1998

In 1998, the Idaho legislature authorized the creation of up to twelve charter schools per year for five years. Schools can either be converted or new. Charters are granted only by local school boards, but if the local board turns down a charter, the initiators can appeal to the state. As of the 1999–2000 school year, there were eight charter schools operating in the state (Center for Education Reform website).

Illinois 1996

Illinois legislation of 1996 permits up to forty-five charter schools: fifteen may be created by the city of Chicago, fifteen may be created in the suburbs around Chicago, and fifteen may be created in the rest of the state. The state has an appeal process if a local board denies a charter. Illinois has a limited appeals process that involves one review. Charter schools are independent legal entities and may contract with staff at school sites with regard to employment and wages. As of the 1999–2000 school year, Illinois had nineteen charter schools (Center for Education Reform website).

Kansas 1994

Kansas legislation passed in 1994 permits up to fifteen charter schools. They must be approved by both the local and the state board of education, and there is no appeals process in the event that a local board turns down a charter application. Kansas does not grant automatic waivers from state education laws and regulations; the waivers must be applied for individually. Kansas charters are granted for specific terms under performance-based contracts. As of the 1999–2000 school year, Kansas had fifteen charter schools operating in the state (Center for Education Reform website).

Louisiana 1995

In 1995, the Louisiana legislature authorized up to forty-two charter schools and permitted an appeal to the state board of education in the event that a local board turns down a charter application. A charter may be for a new school or for a converted school. In the case of a conversion, at least two-thirds of the full-time faculty and instructional staff members must sign a conversion petition along with at least two-thirds of the parents present at a public meeting to discuss the idea. Louisiana charter schools are independent legal entities and can negotiate with staff directly regarding employment and wages. There is no appeals process for denied charters. In 1999, there were seventeen charter schools in the state (Center for Education Reform website).

Massachusetts 1994

Originally authorizing up to twenty-five charter schools, the Massachusetts legislature has changed the law to permit an additional twelve state-authorized charter schools and thirteen new "Horace Mann" charter schools. The latter are schools authorized by a local school board using a contract approved by the local teachers' union. Massachusetts has no appeals process for denied charters, it does not grant automatic waivers from state education laws and regulations, and it does not provide for a process to obtain waivers. The charter schools are legal entities that can contract and negotiate directly with staffs. As of the 1999–2000 school year, Massachusetts had thirty-nine charter schools in operation (Center for Education Reform website).

Michigan 1993

In 1993, the Michigan legislature made it possible for individual local districts, regional district cooperatives, and public universities to sponsor charter schools—the public universities may sponsor a total of seventy-five charter schools. Charter schools are under the supervision of the Michigan State Board of Education. Any group wishing to start a charter school must ask the local community for permission, and a public vote decides whether a charter proposal will be considered. If the vote is no, the idea cannot go forward. If the vote is yes, the idea must be submitted to the local school board in the district in which the school wishes to operate. In Michigan, there is no appeals process for denied charters, but when a charter is denied, the initiator may petition to have the issue placed on the next election ballot. There are no automatic waivers from state education laws and regulations. Michigan charters are contracted for a term based on performance. As of the 1999–2000 school year, Michigan had 175 charter schools (Center for Education Reform website).

Minnesota 1991

In Minnesota, local boards, state boards, and state colleges and universities may sponsor charter schools. When a charter is denied, the state board of education handles the appeal. Minnesota charter schools are legal entities and can negotiate directly with staff regarding employment and wages. Schools are chartered for a specific term, and the contracts are based on performance. As of the 1999–2000 school year, Minnesota had fifty-seven charter schools (Center for Education Reform website).

Nevada 1997

A 1997 Nevada law permits twenty-one charter schools throughout the state. Only local boards have the authority to authorize such schools, and the local boards must first get permission from the state board of education. The current law permits only new schools to be chartered—no conversions are allowed. As of the 1999–2000 school year, Nevada had five charter schools operating within the state (Center for Education Reform website).

New Hampshire 1995

New Hampshire passed charter legislation in 1995. Local boards have the right to sponsor charter schools in the state. If a charter is denied, an appeal can be taken to the state board of education. New Hampshire grants automatic waivers to charter schools, and the schools are considered legal independent entities. They are contracted for a term based on performance. As of 1999, New Hampshire had no charter schools in operation (Center for Education Reform website).

New Jersey 1996

New Jersey legislation from 1996 permits up to 135 charter schools with a maximum of three per county. All of the schools must be approved by the state commissioner of education. Newly created charter schools do not have to follow local labor-management agreements, but charters converted from existing public schools must do so. Regulations may be waived only by petition. New Jersey charter schools are independent legal entities that are contracted for a term based on performance. As of the 1999–2000 school year, New Jersey had fifty-two charter schools (Center for Education Reform website).

New Mexico 1993

The 1993 New Mexico law allows for the establishment of up to five charter schools. Only existing public schools can be converted, and at least 65 percent of the existing school's faculty must vote in favor of the charter application. Parent involvement in the discussion and adoption of the charter school plan must be documented. Teachers remain employees of their local districts, and waivers from state education laws and regulations may be obtained by request. New Mexico does not specify whether charters can negotiate directly with staff, nor has it specified whether charter schools are legal entities. As of 1999, New Mexico had three charter schools (Center for Education Reform website).

New York 1998

As of 1998, the state of New York was still debating its charter school legislation. Still, there were three charter schools operating in the state in 1998. As of October 1999, ninety separate groups had applied to operate charter schools (Center for Education Reform website and Goodnough 1999).

North Carolina 1996

In North Carolina, legislation of 1996 permits local school boards, the state board of education, and the University of North Carolina to sponsor charter schools. The charter legislation allows for both the creation of new schools and the conversion of existing ones. Appeals of charters are handled by the state board of education. Automatic waiver of most state education laws and regulations is granted, and charter schools may negotiate directly with their staffs regarding employment and salaries. Charter schools in North Carolina are considered to be independent legal entities. In 1999, North Carolina had eighty-three charter schools in operation (Center for Education Reform website).

Ohio 1997

The Ohio 1997 charter law allows for both new schools and conversions. Local school boards authorize the charters, and a large number of charters have been authorized in the state's largest cities. As of the 1999–2000 school year, Ohio had forty-eight charter schools operating within the state (Center for Education Reform website).

Oklahoma 1999

In 1999, Oklahoma passed charter school legislation, making it the most recent of all states to have done so. As of 1999, it had no charter schools in operation (Center for Education Reform website).

Oregon 1999

Oregon, too, is one of the latest states to pass legislation for charter schools, also doing so in 1999. As of the 1999–2000 school year, the state had one charter school (Center for Education Reform website).

Pennsylvania 1997

The Pennsylvania legislature actually authorized funds to help individuals and groups plan charter schools, and in 1997, it then authorized an unlimited number of charter schools. Local school boards are the only entities that can sponsor charter schools, and advocates have the right to appeal to the state if a local board turns them down. Any appeal to the state requires the gathering of at least 1,000 signatures of district residents or 2 percent of the district's residents, whichever is fewer. As of the 1999–2000 school year, there were forty-five charter schools operating in the state (Center for Education Reform website).

Rhode Island 1995

Rhode Island's 1995 approach to charter school law gives groups of public personnel the opportunity to create new schools and enables existing public schools to convert to charter status. Two-thirds of the personnel in a given school must approve the conversion of an existing school. If the charter school is to be a new school, at least two-thirds of the number of teachers expected to teach there and one-half of the parents of eligible children must support the school. A charter school proposal first goes to the local school board and then to the state board of regents. The regents (much like a board of education) have the ultimate say as to whether the charter shall be granted. Charter applicants must ask for waivers of local and state regulations in their proposal, and charter school employees remain part of the collective bargaining unit for all teachers in the district. The state board of regents, with the approval of the commissioner and/or local boards, has the right to grant a charter. There is no appeal process in the event a charter is denied. Rhode Island does not automatically grant waivers from state education laws and regulations, but waivers may be requested. The state does not allow its charter schools to negotiate directly with staffs, and the schools are not legal entities under the law. Rhode Island charters are granted for a specific term under a performance-based contract. In 1999, Rhode Island had two charter schools (Center for Education Reform website).

South Carolina 1996

According to 1996 legislation, only local school boards can authorize charter schools in the state of South Carolina. Both new schools and converted public school plans are permitted. The state board may listen to an appeal but may not actually grant a charter. For newly started charter schools, employment and salaries may be negotiated directly with staffs; that is not the case for conversions. Charter schools are contracted on term-based performance contracts and are considered to be independent entities. In 1999 South Carolina had ten charter schools (Center for Education Reform website).

Texas 1995

Texas legislative action in 1995 allowed the state to charter up to 120 schools. The state may also sponsor an unlimited number of charter schools that plan to have at least 75 percent of their students be at risk of failure. Texas allows local districts to establish new schools that are exempt from most state education laws and rules. Called campus or program charters, district-sponsored schools are operating throughout the state. There are no appeals when a charter is denied. Charter schools are contracted under performance-based contracts for a specific term and presumably are considered to be independent legal entities. It is not specified in the legislation governing charter schools in Texas whether those schools may contract directly with employees. As of the 1999–2000 school year, Texas had 168 charter schools (Center for Education Reform website).

Utah 1998

In 1998, Utah legislators authorized the creation of up to eight charter schools, which can be either new schools or conversions. The Utah State Board of Education is the authorizing body with responsibility for chartering schools. In 1999, Utah had eight charter schools (Center for Education Reform website).

Virginia 1998

Only local school boards can charter schools in Virginia. Charter legislation, adopted by the state in 1998, states that until June 2000 no more than two charters may be granted per district. Beginning 1 June 2000, the number of charter schools shall not exceed 10 percent of the total number of schools in a district or two schools, whichever is greater. As of 1999, Virginia had no charter schools (Center for Education Reform website).

Wisconsin 1993

Local school boards are the only entities that can sponsor and authorize a charter school in Wisconsin except in Milwaukee. That city's city council was granted power by the legislature in 1993 to authorize charter schools. In Milwaukee, charter schools may negotiate directly with employees regarding wages and conditions, and it is only there that charter schools are considered to be independent legal entities. As of the 1999–2000 school year, Wisconsin had forty-five charter schools operating in the state (Center for Education Reform website).

Wyoming 1995

According to 1995 legislation, only local school boards may sponsor charter schools in Wyoming. In order to establish a charter school, a person must have a petition signed by at least 10 percent of the teachers employed by the district or at least 50 percent of the teachers employed at one school site in the district. The petition must also be signed by at least 10 percent of the parents of all pupils in the district or by at least 50 percent of the parents of all pupils enrolled at one school in the district. There is no appeals process in Wyoming. It is not specified whether charter schools receive an automatic waiver of education laws and regulations, nor is it specified whether they are to be independent legal entities with the right to contract directly with employees. As of the 1999–2000 school year, Wyoming had no charter schools (Center for Education Reform website).

Nationwide

Nationwide, as of the 1999–2000 school year, 1,682 charter schools were open and operating across all fifty states and the District of Columbia (Center for Education Reform website).

STARTING A CHARTER SCHOOL

Even though laws regarding charter school laws differ from state to state, charter school developers usually proceed through the same rudimentary steps when looking to create a charter school. Starting such a school is relatively easy, but there are some things that should be kept in mind when thinking about starting one. As examples, Appendix A provides an application submitted by the Mater Center School in Florida, and Appendix B provides the articles of incorporation filed by that school.

Doing a Situational Analysis

The first thing charter school developers must do is think about the reasons they and others wish to start a charter school—what their goals, missions, and objectives are and how they plan to accomplish them. It is important to have clear and precise reasons as to why one is even contemplating the idea. From there, one should begin to gather the necessary background information to help in the design process. For example, one needs to review the state law, assemble a team that can share the responsibilities for beginning the school, look at some other charter schools in the state, and design a framework for how to proceed. Because the charter school laws are mercurial and change considerably over small amounts of time, it is advisable to investigate how the laws in the state might have changed.

A state's charter law defines who may grant a charter, and it is important to look at the granting agency to determine if certain rules and guidelines must be followed in the submission of the charter proposal. The guidelines can help make thoughts regarding the charter school more specific as well as help prepare one for the necessary legal work and other paperwork involved.

An informal plan can be put together, one that is not specifically detailed but provides a general direction, or one can proceed with a more complicated and detailed strategic plan. It is important to think about funding at this point and perhaps even look for some start-up funds from either public or private sources. Looking at foundations that provide grants could be a useful way to proceed.

Assembling a Core Group of True Believers

It is necessary to put together an organizing group, the group that will move the idea from imagination to actual reality. This group will write the charter, and some of the members might even operate the school. Careful thought should go into thinking about whom to include in the organizing group. The organizing group will need expertise in at least the following areas:

- Curriculum and instruction
- Community relations and marketing

- Finance and fund-raising
- Governance and management
- Legal issues and school law
- Real estate issues of where to locate
- Student assessment
- Writing charter and grant documents

The key to putting together a core or organizing group is to draw together diverse people from various walks of life. It might be useful to include community leaders, professional workers, blue-collar workers, parents, educators, entrepreneurs, and people with vision and imagination, and it is necessary to identify key people who might serve as a resource such as parents, business people, community leaders, and management experts.

Designing the Plan

Once the organizing group has been assembled, it is time to think in terms of designing a plan for realization. The original idea may be a good one, but until it is fleshed out and implemented, it will remain a dream. Some of the issues that must be considered in the start-up design or plan are:

- A mission and vision statement
- An overview of curricular goals
- A description of the day-to-day operation of the school and its governance
- A statement of facility needs
- A preliminary budget

In reviewing the mission statement of a number of charters, the Consortium for Policy Research in Education at Pennsylvania State University found that although the charter schools it studied varied in terms of student population, level of schooling, and whether they were new schools or conversions, the school missions were similar. Wording such as "preparing students for the twenty-first century" or "what it means to be an educated person in the twenty-first century" was common in the mission statements (Wohlstetter and Griffin 1997, 11). Technology preparedness and consideration of students' emotional needs were also found to be themes in the mission statements of the schools studied.

The study also found that although a broad and general mission statement may be helpful when seeking approval for the charter, broadly defined, generalized missions are not helpful in providing specific directions regarding teaching and learning. In one start-up middle school studied, the consortium found that the school's mission was so vague that approaches to math instruction were being used differently by different teachers (Wohlstetter and Griffin 1997, 11). Thus, the mission statement that is drafted should be broad enough to gain wide appeal and allow for diversity in style yet specific enough to allow the statement to serve as a guide for specific teaching principles and methods of learning.

No school can become a charter school until its charter is approved. In order to gain approval, the charter must be written and the charter-granting agency applied to. When writing the charter, it is a good idea to procure a charter for a similar school in the area that has already been approved (see also Appendix A). Other applications can act as benchmarks and allow the people writing the charter to see what is necessary and important to highlight or emphasize. Some key components of solid charter applications are:

- Clear mission and vision statement
- Statement of why such a school is needed
- Description of the educational program to be used and the curricular approaches
- Descriptive methods of assessment
- Personnel policies
- Student policies, including discipline
- Financial plan for the school
- Learning objectives and connection with state standards
- Governance of the school

Having a well-articulated and integrated instructional program is key for successful charter applications, and having a consistent and content-based professional development program for staff members is crucial for implementation. In its study of start-up and conversion charters, the Consortium for Policy Research in Education at Pennsylvania State University found that buying or adopting an educational instruction system was not enough for the charter schools studied. What was needed, the study concluded, was an ongoing, school-wide professional development program that encouraged development and dialogue around curricular issues and concerns (Wohlstetter and Griffin 1997, 21). Quick-fix, formula-based approaches to learning and teaching are too simplistic and divorce the conception of teaching from its practice. In writing the charter, it is necessary to consider how the school will provide professional development time, funding, and formal structures for teacher collaboration and personal growth.

One should also make sure that there are formal accountability systems and standards in place for assessing student achievement. These should include multiple assessments. It is also important to make sure one fully understands the state assessment requirements. The Consortium for Policy Research in Education also found in its study of numerous charter schools not only that formal systems of accountability were lacking at most of the schools they studied but that without clear directions from the state, most of the charter schools had to draw on their own organizational capacities to generate accountability plans, and few of the schools had a strong enough capacity to do so. Accountability problems can be avoided by ensuring that that are clear and definitive structures set up to measure student performance, which means that everyone involved will need a clear and accurate understanding of the state standards and the curriculum goals that will be used to meet them.

Gaining Approval for the Charter

After the charter has been drafted and key components have been addressed, it is time to get the charter approved. It is important to first circulate the draft of the charter to community leaders and any other interested parties that have been identified. Their feedback should be elicited, and changes in the draft should be made if it is felt such changes are warranted. It is also important to get information about the charter-granting agency in order to know what the agency is looking for and what it has done in the past in terms of granting or denying charters. Look at other charters they have approved and be prepared to show how the school being applied for will meet the specifically detailed needs that have been identified.

After Approval: Opening the School

After the charter is approved, it is time to actually begin to set up the school, and it is important to pay particular attention to some of the basic navigating issues for this phase of the school. At a minimum, pay attention to

- Developing a detailed plan for all the tasks that need to be done once the school opens its doors. Tasks and responsibilities should be delegated and understood by the core organizing group and others who will be involved in the daily operation of the school.

- Developing some agreements with the sponsoring district, its servers and providers, to assure that they will provide needed services.
- Formalizing the instructional program. Get the needed materials and resources, discuss them, and have them available the first day the school opens.
- If nonprofit status is being considered, procuring the materials or legal advice needed to begin and legalizing the nonprofit organization with the government.
- Making sure the facility services, such as food, transportation if provided, and other services, are in place.

Once issues involving the school have been thought about and the inevitable first day of opening has been planned for, the school's doors are ready to be opened. Everyone involved must work hard to establish a culture for the school, set up lines of communication, assure that student performance issues and reporting requirements are met, collect information and data to justify the school's continued existence, and begin troubleshooting—especially looking for ways to improve the school. Some areas of concern:

- Have an opening date for the school and work to establish and maintain a culture
- Implement the designs and procedures and consistently review them for monitoring purposes
- Look for gaps and unforeseen problems in the operation procedure
- Monitor and refine the curriculum and instruction
- Develop good problem-solving procedures and identify problems and subproblems that may arise
- Make sure data on the school are constantly collected in order to support rationales and to plan for the future

If good planning and effective organization are emphasized in the early stages, the success of the charter school will be far more secure. Good planning, competent teamwork, and effective delegation of authority and tasks can assure that the charter school operates effectively and competently.

Developing, Enabling, and Sustaining a Learning Community

Developing, enabling, and sustaining the learning community are all crucial, for charter schools are successes or failures depending on the learning environment. Some issues to consider when making sure that the school environment is one of learning and development are:

- Autonomy—The amount of autonomy a charter school has seems to have a great deal to do with its ability to sustain a learning community (Wohlstetter and Griffin 1997, 34). Whether or not a school can avail itself of community resources; maintain control of budgetary issues; develop autonomy from the district office; and be able to set its own agenda, craft its own curricular approaches, and select and adopt curriculum programs has a lot to do with sustaining a learning community.
- Having the organizational capacity to develop programs.
- Networking—Organizations that support charter schools have begun all over the United States. Linking up with these organizations can be crucial to a charter school's ability to sustain its learning community. Networking with state, local, and regional organizations can help a charter school develop and sustain a learning environment. These organizations can offer anything from curriculum ideas to funding conduits.
- Parental involvement—Supportive parents who are actively engaged in the mission and vision of the charter school can make the difference between success and failure. Setting up focus groups, governing mechanisms, and structural approaches to elicit and maintain parental involvement is crucial. Parental involvement can make many different things happen, from financial support to providing food at staff meetings. Knowing that parents are involved and can be counted on for support can set staff members at ease and allow them to form collaborative partnerships with students, the administration, and parents.
- Continually revisiting and reflecting on the performance of the school with all stakeholders. Such action is necessary to craft and sustain a learning community at a charter school. Dialogue and communication in an atmosphere of civility and inquiry can assure a charter school's success even in the face of some difficult problems.

Building support with the community and working well with all participants at the school will help assure the school's success and development. Continually identifying problems and working toward common solutions will ensure that the school is engaged in self-assessment for continual improvement.

REFERENCES

Center for Education Reform website. 30 December 1999. http://edreform. com.

Christoff, Chris. "Engler Must Build Coalition to Pass Bold School Changes." *Detroit Free Press,* 5 October 1993.

———. "Stabenow Unveils Plan for Schools." *Detroit Free Press,* 16 September 1993.

Council of Urban Boards of Education. *The Basics of Charter Schools.* Alexandria, VA: National School Boards Association, 1997.

Engler, John. "Our Kids Deserve Better: New Schools for a New Century." Report from Office of the Governor of Michigan, 1993.

Finn, Chester E., Jr., Bruno Manno, and Louann Bierlein. *Charter Schools in Action: What Have We Learned?* Washington, DC: Hudson Institute, 1997.

Goodnough, A. "90 Groups Apply to Operate Charter Schools," *New York Times,* 26 October 1999, Metropolitan Desk Section.

Hassel, Bryan. *The Charter School Challenge.* Washington, DC: Brookings Institute, 1999.

———. *The Charter School Challenge: Avoiding the Pitfalls, Fulfilling the Promise.* Washington, DC: Brookings Institute, 1995.

Kolderie, Ted. *The Charter Idea: Update and Prospects, Fall 1995.* Public Services Redesign Project. St. Paul, MN: Center for Policy Studies, 1995.

Manno, Bruno, et al. "Charter School Accountability: Problems and Prospects." Pt. 4 of Chester E. Finn, Jr., Bruce Manno, and Louann Bierlein, *Charter Schools in Action: What Have We Learned?* Washington, DC: Hudson Institute, 1997.

"Metro News Briefs: New Jersey Supreme Court to Hear Charter School Suit." *New York Times,* 30 December 1999.

Molnar, Alex. "Charter Schools: The Smiling Face of Disinvestment." *Educational Leadership* 54, no. 2 (October 1996): 1–9.

Nathan, Joe. *Charter Schools: Creating Hope and Opportunity for American Education.* San Francisco: Jossey-Bass, 1996.

Nelson, E. H. "How Much Thirty Thousand Charter Schools Cost." Paper presented on behalf of the American Federation of Teachers at the annual meeting of the American Education Finance Association, Jacksonville, FL, March 1997.

Premack, Eric. "Charter Schools: California's Education Reform 'Power Tool.'" *Phi Delta Kappan* 78, no. 1 (September 1996): 60–64.

University of Minnesota Humphrey Institute of Public Affairs and Education Commission of the States. *Charter Schools: What Are They Up To? A 1995 Survey.* Denver: Education Commission of the States, 1996.

Vergari, Sandra. "School Finance Reform in the State of Michigan." *Journal of Educational Finance* 21 (1995): 254–270.

Wohlstetter, P., and N. Griffin. *Creating and Sustaining Learning Communities: Early Lessons from Charter Schools.* Philadelphia: Consortium for Policy Research in Education, 1997.

Chapter Five

❧ Politics and the Charter School Challenge

HISTORICAL BACKGROUND

Any understanding of the politics of the charter school reform movement, its recent emergence, challenges, and promises, must be understood within the sociohistorical context that spawned it. Charter schools are a unique and historical educational reform concept with deep roots in important historical controversies over the purposes of education, educational funding, the role of education in market societies, morality, cultural hegemony, race, gender, and social class. Unfortunately, as educational author and reformer Herbert Kliebard has lamented, movements for school change generally fail to understand the history of educational reform in the United States. According to Kliebard, "New breakthroughs are solemnly proclaimed when in fact they represent minor modifications of early proposals, and, conversely, anachronistic dogmas and doctrines maintain a currency and uncritical acceptance far beyond their present merit" (Kliebard 1970, 259). Kliebard called upon educators to examine new and popular school reform proposals from a historical perspective. For our purposes, this historical examination will specifically focus on the historical development of education as it affected and still affects the growth and maturing of charter schools as a reform movement.

We begin our understanding of the politics of charter schools by briefly exploring the historical origins of some of the controversies popular in educational discourses today. We also look at the rise of public schooling in the United States from the late nineteenth century up to, and including, the present. This period of time includes the industrial revolution, the urbanization of the United States, the development of modernism, and the current situation in postindustrial United States—all historical developments and issues that affect charter schools.

The historical treatment of these epochs in the United States is not intended to be exhaustive but is designed instead to be illustrative of the forces that have given rise to the current political climate, terms, and level of debate regarding charter school reform in education in the United States today. By placing the charter school concept under the

95

critical lens of historical scrutiny, we can better understand charter schools as a contemporary educational reform movement: a movement born as the result of specific, cultural, economic, and historical relations and forces. With this understanding, we will be in a better position to acquire a deeper and richer comprehension of the contemporary politics that configure the current controversy over charter schools and therefore in a better position to assess their strengths and merits.

American Industrialism and the Factory School

The end of the American Civil War in 1865 and the immediate years that followed brought unbridled economic growth and development to the country. New scientific and technological developments fueled the expansion of markets and shaped a deeply changing country. More and more Americans began to live in large urban centers, which led to the increased development and expansion of cities. Coupled with immigration, the increased urbanization and industrialization of the late nineteenth and early twentieth centuries led to a rapid growth of U.S. industry and a new concentration of economic power in the hands of emerging industrialists and corporations.

Immigration helped the political and cultural landscape of the country in the late 1800s as larger urban centers were not only growing but for the first time were growing with people other than white Anglos (Kincheloe 2000, 151). Along with this rapid growth there was a need to assimilate the new immigrants into the melting pot of "mainstream" American life. An obvious and logical forum for this assimilation was the public school. Work in urban centers during this time in history was largely relegated to factory work, so the first public schools in the United States resembled the factory as well. There were bells to sound the beginning of classes, desks were bolted to the floor in regimented rows, strict discipline was maintained, and there was a rigidly imposed social order (Kincheloe 2000, 152).

The costs of building these new factory-type schools were justified in the minds of the public by appeals to the "national interest." The argument was simple: immigrant children were in the United States because the United States needed the labor of their parents to become rich and prosperous. The market rationale at the time also argued that educating these children would lead to a positive return on investment, that is, a more productive workforce and a more competitive country. One leading educational reformer at the time, Ellwood Cubberley, wrote: "Our schools are, in a sense, factories in which the raw products (children) are to be shaped and fashioned into products to meet the demands of life. The specifications for manufacturing come from the demands of twentieth century civilization, and it is the business of the school to build its pupils according to the specifications laid down" (Cubberley 1916, 338).

If the public school represented the factory, the students themselves were little more than the raw material or objects of production; they were products to be fashioned by the public school system. In the emerging modern public schools of the United States, children, especially immigrant children, were to be trained to follow directions and routines, learn proper English, and develop rudimentary "basic skills" such as reading, mathematics, and writing. Schooling, in a sense, developed as a center for socialization and indoctrination as the United States entered the industrial era.

In the post–Civil War United States, market interests and business concerns rapidly permeated public schools. Not only was the curriculum of the public schools immersed in the growth, regulation, and maintenance of urbanization and the rise of industrialization and factory existence, the schools were also implicated in the development of a modernist conception of knowledge and intelligence. When we examine charter school politics in depth, we will see that this marriage, the marriage between market interests and public education, is one of the most controversial aspects of charter school reform.

Between 1880 and 1920, as the factory-style public school system emerged, so, too, did the philosophy which specified that the reality and life of both students and teachers needed to be scientifically oriented and regulated (Kincheloe 2000, 153). Standardized tests began during this period, and emphasis in the tests was on sorting and categorizing mechanisms that would place students on specific curricular tracks. Modern rationalism and specific, linear ways of knowing emerged as the measure of intelligence, and the new standardized tests, such as the Stanford Benet Test, were designed to calibrate and classify students based on emerging modernist notions of intellectual behavior. These instruments of assessment also gave specific direction to teachers as to what they should be doing in their classrooms, how they should organize their time and priorities, and what subjects should be emphasized.

The burgeoning industrial capitalism of the late 1800s and early 1900s needed schools to preserve, extend, and legitimize the economic relations of production and the arrival of new forms of unprecedented consumption. Consequently, during this period, there was the rise and development of an educational philosophy called social functionalism: education organized, implemented, and controlled to meet the functional needs of society's business and economic interests. These functional needs became increasingly identified with what was necessary in the workplace, and as we shall see, controversies regarding social functionalism were one of the impetuses that encouraged the growth of charter schools.

Directly associated with the social functionalism of schools was an excessive preoccupation with the values of productivity, efficiency, and thrift (Goodman 1995, 6). With the development of the assembly line and specifically the contributions of Frederick Taylor to the new science of business management that was being realized on assembly lines, efficiency, productivity, and speed began to capture the imagination of the American public. Factory work relied on workers who could follow instructions, understand simple directions, and work swiftly to increase production with maximum efficiency. With the small shopkeeper disappearing and corporate power beginning to emerge, the industrialist and the industrial tycoon now became the cultural model for a successful person (Huber 1971). Industrial production proceeded at levels unheard of before, and the power and ideology of industrialized production became the infatuation and ideology of the United States during this period.

It is hard not to see the parallel between that historical time period and today. Although contemporary production has shifted to technological and service work as the United States enters into the "third wave" of postindustrialism, infatuation with technological tycoons, cybernet billionaires, and the ideology of efficiency and "lean production" now dominates the country's culture. School-to-work programs are important aspects of many public schools, and charter schools have arisen partly in response to the demands of the new social functionalism and the proclaimed need to prepare students for the exigencies of production in the twenty-first century. Some charter schools have also arisen as a result of general opposition to this idea.

The social functionalism prevalent in the philosophy of early-twentieth-century educational discourse, along with a preoccupation for speed and efficiency, was described by the then-leading reformer Franklin Bobbitt, one of the key social functionalists for the school restructuring movement during the industrial age. Bobbitt claimed as early as 1924:

> It is helpful to begin with the simple assumption to be accepted literally, that education is to prepare men and women for the activities of adult life; and that nothing should be included which does not serve this purpose. . . . The first task is to discover the activities which ought to make up the lives of men and women; and along with these, the abilities and personal qualities necessary for proper performance. These

are educational objectives. When we know what men and women ought to do then we shall have before us the things for which they should be trained. (Bobbitt 1912, 259–271)

The activities to which Bobbitt referred were tied to necessities that resulted from changes in the relations of production and consumption that were exploding at the time.

Not only did the industrial age have an impact on the purposes and goals of education, but the social functionalism of the time also affected staffing patterns, curriculum construction, and instructional design (Goodman 1995, 6). What Raymond Callahan referred to as the "cult" of efficiency and productivity had an effect on every aspect of schooling (Callahan 1962). Taylorism (named for Frederick Taylor, the father of the assembly line), the modern science of business management, was rapidly being implemented in school production. With educational goals being restructured and defined as increasing productivity in schools, in essence the quantity rather than the quality of what students learn, the factory school began to predetermine outcomes and then plan backward to restructure education so that those outcomes could be reached. Bobbitt described this process as early as 1913:

> The third grade teacher should bring her pupils up to an average of 26 correct combinations in addition per minute. The fourth grade teacher has the task, during the year that the same pupils are under her care, of increasing their addition speed from an average of 26 combinations per minute to an average of 34 combinations per minute. If she does not bring them up to the standard 34, she has failed to perform her duty in proportion to the deficit; and there is no responsibility beyond the standard. (Bobbitt 1913, 21–22)

Specifically stated learning objectives that could be measured, controlled, and regulated became the language of the modernist's educational discourse. These objectives were tied to what was needed or what was divined to be functional in the new industrial society that was emerging. With an "objectives first" approach to education and schooling, curricula underwent unique changes. Not only were educators at the time concerned with efficiency and production, they also believed strongly in the practice of differentiated staffing (Goodman 1995, 10). Knowledge acquisition was fragmented into disciplines and subjects, much like the work on the assembly lines in the industrial factories. Conception of education was divorced from its execution. Thus, a fragmented curriculum and "teacher specialists" developed.

The important goal for the social functionalists and efficiency educators of the day was to reduce the number of educational workers by maximizing their instructional efficiency. Thus, not unlike what Taylor advocated for the factory, no one person was to ever be responsible for too many different tasks. Scientism and the instrumentalist approaches of the functionalist educators divided teaching up into distinct and differentiated tasks staffed by distinct individuals.

The reconfiguration of the school day and the redesign of curriculum during the industrial revolution in the early part of the twentieth century helped shape what we now know as the large, factory-style urban public school and the public school curriculum. As we shall see, Bobbitt's appeal to link school to work was not much different than positions taken by certain educational policymakers and business leaders today. And in the same way that Taylorism and the new science of business administration influenced the conception and organization of schooling during the early twentieth century, contemporary changes in production, consumption, and business management theory continue to exert a tremendous influence on the public school debate today. This, in turn, is reflected in the debate regarding school choice and the charter school reform movement.

African Americans and the Factory School

With the emergence of the factory school, educating children for the responsibilities associated with public citizenship was increasingly sacrificed for the quantitative imperatives of the newly emerging industrial society and capitalist market. The purposes of education were deeply connected to the necessities of efficiency and productivity. School administrators at the time even began to think of themselves as "school executives" rather than as educators of children (Callahan 1962). Educational language changed as the vocabulary of business was adopted to describe education and schools. Another leading reformer and educational functionalist at the time, Ellwood Cubberley, asserted a vocabulary of business when expressing the need for educational efficiency and production:

> Every manufacturing establishment that turns out a standard product ... maintains a force of efficiency experts to study methods of procedure to measure and test the output of its workers. Such men ultimately bring the manufacturing establishment large returns, by introducing improvements in processes and procedure, and in training the workmen to produce larger and better output. ... In time, it will be

possible for any school system to maintain a continuous survey of all of the different phases of its work, through tests made by its corps of efficiency experts, and to detect weak points in its work almost as soon as they appear. (Cubberley 1916, 338)

Yet the historical reality of the emerging factory school, with its social functionalism and cult of efficiency, produced a quandary for many African American children. The questions at issue that both the black community and the white Anglo community were to wrestle with during this period involved the purposes of education, whom it should serve, who should have access to it, and why. This debate was most evident in the African American community in the decades that followed reconstruction.

Two powerful and contrasting African American leaders at the time expressed profoundly different ideas as to the purposes for educating black children. Booker T. Washington stressed the necessity of agrarian and vocational education for African American children. In the spirit of social functionalism, he felt the role of schools was to teach children a trade or useful skill they might use in the larger white-controlled society. An ex-slave, Washington, much like the social functionalists Bobbitt and Cubberley, felt that education should be prepare one for future work. His prescription to blacks in the South is useful to consider for it summed up succinctly his view on education and education al purpose: "Make yourself useful to the south; be honest, be thrifty; cultivate the white man's friendliness; above all, educate your children and prepare them for the future" (Perkinson 1989, 49).

W. E. B. DuBois, unlike Washington and his social functionalist contemporaries, felt that the overriding purpose and goal behind the education of African American children was to educate them for full citizenship in American society, not simply for the needs of a segregated and white market civilization. Although Washington stressed economic pragmatism as the chief consideration in defining educational purpose, DuBois argued that African American children should be educated in the tradition of the liberal arts, the necessities of responsible and moral leadership, and participation in democracy. He felt that the role of education "is not to make carpenters out of men, but men out of carpenters" (DuBois 1973, 52). And while Washington believed that African Americans could not achieve full citizenship until they were economically self-sufficient, DuBois believed that education itself was the key to full citizenship, not simply a means to economic self-sufficiency. DuBois declared in 1906: "We claim for ourselves every single right that belongs to a freeborn American, political, civil, and social; and until we get these rights we will never cease to protest and assail the ears of America" (DuBois 1924, 53).

Controversies in the black community over the purposes of education, social functionalism, and the role of culture in schooling are arguably more complex issues today than they were during the time of Washington and DuBois. The Washington-DuBois debates, although heated and controversial at the time, were concerned with the goals of education for African Americans during a time when education was adapting to an emerging industrial society. Similarly, today we see these controversies reflected in the emerging cybernetic revolution as educational goals are debated in a rapidly changing technological and social environment. Similar struggles for access to educational excellence and equal opportunity emerge now, as they did during the Washington-DuBois debates.

Washington's vision of schooling prevailed over that of the more visionary DuBois. Yet it is important to note that the discussion concerning educational purpose continues unabated in the black community. With the advent of charter schools, this debate now takes on different proportions and levels of complexity as charters have the ability to serve various philosophical tenets.

Progressive Educational Responses to the Factory School

Although the factory style of education during the latter part of the nineteenth century and the early part of the twentieth imposed a functionalistic, industrial education on all U.S. citizens—African American, Native American, newly arriving immigrants, and Anglos—it was not without its critics and staunch opponents. Even though the prevailing wisdom at the time argued for impersonal factory schools grounded on modernist approaches to curriculum and teaching, many educators protested. They not only saw the factory school as an impersonal social arrangement, they saw industrial society and the factory life that was emerging as an impediment to human development. Margaret Haley, a union organizer and teacher-activist at the time, expressed the following:

> Two ideals are struggling for supremacy in American life today; one the industrial ideal, dominating through the supremacy of commercialism, which subordinates the worker to the product, and the machine; the other ideal of democracy, the ideal of educators, which places humanity above all machines, and demands that all activity shall be the expression of life. (Tyack 1974, 257)

Educators like Haley opposed what they viewed as the rigid and impersonal social order imposed by the capitalist relations of factory life. She, like many of her contemporaries, felt that the rise of corporations and corporate power were far more menacing to life in the United States than was the role of government (Kincheloe 2000, 159). These educational progressives wanted schools to provide educational experiences for children that expanded their involvement in citizenship activities and civic responsibility, and to this end they argued that public education must construct its own mission and purpose. They viewed education as a vehicle for human freedom, emancipation, and democratic citizenship—not simply a means to an economic end.

Besides DuBois and Haley, another prominent progressive educator and philosopher during the early part of the twentieth century was John Dewey. Like Haley and other opponents of social functionalism, Dewey argued against reducing schooling to mere functionalism—boring and repetitive tasks designed to prepare students for future work. Dewey's argument against social functionalism maintained that the role and purpose behind education should be to prepare students to live fully in the present, not simply to prepare them for the future. Like Boyd Bode, another progressive educator of the time, Dewey argued that for schooling to be merely a preparatory institution for future market needs was dehumanizing and denied children the opportunity to find relevancy, identity, and meaning in their lives. Dewey commented:

> The ideal of using the present simply to get ready for the future contradicts itself. It omits, and even shuts out, the very conditions by which a person can be prepared for his future. We always live at the time we live and not at some other time, and only by extracting at each present time the full meaning of each present experience are we prepared for doing the same thing in the future. This is the only preparation which in the long run amounts to anything. (Dewey 1976, 49)

Dewey himself was very clear regarding what he and other progressives conceived of as the purpose and objective of education:

> The problem of education in its relation to the direction of social change is all one with the problem of finding out what democracy means in total range of concrete applications; domestic, international, religious, cultural, economic, *and* political. . . . The trouble . . . is that we have taken democracy for granted; we have thought and acted as if our forefathers had founded it once and for all. We have forgotten that it has to be enacted anew with every generation, in every year, in every

day, in the living relations of person to person, in all social forms and institutions. Forgetting this . . . we have been negligent in creating a school that should be the constant nurse of democracy. (Dewey 1940, 357–358)

Dewey was convinced that democracy was not a "thing" that is found, but an idea that is perpetually created. His notion of education rested upon a citizenry concerned with developing the ability to visualize the type of society its members wished to live in and then working collaboratively to create it.

Although the debate between progressive educators like Dewey, Bode, DuBois, and Haley on the one hand and Bobbitt and Cubberley on the other was intense and controversial, in the end, functionalism triumphed over progressivism. There are many reasons for the triumph of social functionalism in the educational debates in the United States during the early part of the twentieth century, not the least being the cost of subsidizing and operating public education as an enterprise. Progressive educational ideas would have required new structural configurations of schools, an emphasis on quality education as opposed to educating quantities of students, new assessments, and more creative and innovative curricula. Social functionalist approaches to education, on the other hand, were less expensive precisely because within the factory style of school, students could be "produced" through educational "formulas" on an educational assembly line in much larger numbers than the craftsmanship required by progressive education (Wirt and Kirst 1992). Education was far more efficient, it was argued, when it was reduced to an ecumenical formula.

Perhaps even more important, the progressive agenda for education was highly controversial and threatened the elite agenda of control and power that was beginning to take shape in industrialized, modernist America. With the emergence of union activism, independent socialist movements—coupled with the creation of the former Soviet Union in 1917 and the so-called Red scare and the Sacco and Vanzetti trial of the 1920s—the last thing that policymakers in education, business, or politics wanted was education for social liberation and individual realization. Business interests, policymakers, and politicians were worried that opening up education to such things as personal awareness, democracy, social exploration, and critical analysis might compel the public to examine the social, cultural, and economic relations that governed their lives. Such a result had the possibility of posing a considerable threat to power, authority, and control and was of little interest to the captains of a market society undergoing a huge economic expansion, technological revolution, rising industrialization, and an unprecedented concentration of wealth. Their notion of education for social function and control was far more pragmatic in an emerging industrial world in which commercialism relied on disciplined workers and irresponsible consumers.

As a result, Dewey's progressive ideas had little support from administrators and other educational policymakers. Thus, the debates between progressives and social functionalists had little practical effect during the early part of the twentieth century, schools were increasingly organized on factory models, and their curricula were increasingly wedded to organizational and intellectual endeavors that promoted education as preparation for work.

Today, many progressive educators and parents who find Dewey's notion of educational purpose important have begun to open charter schools with instructional methodologies and curricula based on progressive educational concerns. For many of these educators, parents, students, and community stakeholders, the charter school reform effort means freedom from the factory style of education. It also means they can now organize, orient, and construct their school vision based on interdisciplinary and progressive ideals and their own brand of philosophy.

The argument between Washington and DuBois and the educational functionalists and educational progressives is as heated today as it was in the beginning of the twentieth century, perhaps even more so. The issues that confronted educators in the early twentieth century—curriculum construction, access to quality education, the education of minority children and newly arriving immigrants, race, gender equity, social class, market capitalism, technological innovation, work, efficiency and production, and the purpose and goals of education—represent similar but different challenges, much as they did close to 100 years ago. The idea of the charter school, or the notion of public school choice, has its roots in the controversies that Washington, DuBois, Haley, Dewey, and their functionalist contemporaries—Bobbitt and Cubberley—engaged in more than seventy-five years ago. These issues help explain the development and demands of charter schools among specific segments and constituencies of the population.

Post–World War II Politics of Public Education

Public education in post–World War II United States involved some most dramatic transformations and challenges in the context of the cold war, McCarthyism, economic prosperity, suburban development, technological innovations in consumer goods, the advent of television and advertising, the growth of the civil rights movement, and the rapid development of scientific innovation and discovery. During this time, controversial and rancorous debates arose over the role of education and universal access to school facilities.

Perhaps the most important event that marked post–World War II social, racial, and educational politics was the 1954 Supreme Court decision *Brown v. Board of Education*. Up to that time, what was referred to as "the separate-but-equal doctrine," upheld in *Plessy v. Ferguson*, had governed relations between blacks and whites. The *Brown* decision overturned *Plessy*, declaring the separate-but-equal doctrine "inherently unequal." In a 1955 follow-up decision, the Court further clarified its position on the matter by stating that public school systems that had been segregated until that time now had to become desegregated *(Brown v. Board of Education II)*.

The Supreme Court decisions also brought up the heated issue of "states rights" versus federal control—an issue as old as the Civil War itself. Many conservative southerners felt that decisions regarding local issues should be left to the states and local government bodies, not be mandated by the federal government. Many conservatives at the time saw the Supreme Court's decision in *Brown v. Board of Education* as a federal invasion of states' rights.

Another important post–World War II event that was to have a massive impact on the nation's school systems and the continued public debate over education was the 1957 advance of the Soviet Union into space with the launching of *Sputnik*. U.S. leaders reacted to that Soviet success with shock and disbelief, arguing that the Soviet Union now had a military advantage over the United States. Business leaders, military leaders, and educational policymakers scrambled to assign the blame to the public schools. Given the permissiveness of the 1950s, in everything from music to new conventions regarding sexuality and conformity, blaming public education for not preparing the United States for global and economic competitiveness was convenient, and attacks on public education intensified with increasing regularity (Kincheloe 2000, 164).

After the launching of *Sputnik* and given the perceived Soviet superiority in matters of technology and military development, the federal government began to become more involved in the legal and economic realities of public education. The National Defense and Education Act was passed, and the educational emphasis now focused primarily on science, mathematics, foreign languages, guidance, career counseling, and vocational endeavors in an effort to compete more effectively with the Soviet Union. The federal government also appropriated and spent massive sums for capital improvements and the construction of schools and buildings.

Worried that the Soviet Union was achieving technological and military dominance over the United States, educational policymakers believed they were the custodians of a public educational system designed to prepare U.S. citizens for the rigorous necessities of economic and military dominance. Education was now to be perceived as a vehicle for gaining the necessary skills for the promotion of "the national interest" and was directly linked to defeating communism at any cost. For the first time in its history, the U.S. government declared education a national preoccupation and a national interest, and linking U.S. readiness to educational standards became the talk of the day. The public schools were still organized like large factories, but they were now factories that were more preoccupied with the regulation of the curriculum in the interests of national sovereignty and economic readiness. In this atmosphere of political fear and stated educational purpose tied to military and technological preparedness, the voices of educational progressives, like Dewey and DuBois, were muted.

The efforts to promote an educational marketplace through privatized school choice can be traced directly to the work of the conservative economist Milton Friedman in the 1950s. Unlike proponents of public education who sought restructuring and reform of factory-style public schools, Friedman proposed in 1955 that every family be given a federal "voucher" to be used for each child attending any school—public or private. Under the proposed plan, the voucher would be paid for by public funds and would allow families to select a school of their choice that met minimal governmental oversight. Parents could also add their own resources to the value of the voucher, and each school would operate like a business, setting its own tuition and admission requirements (Friedman 1955).

Not only did Friedman's proposal fail to attract public interest at the time, the prevailing ideology argued that a simple retooling of the curriculum and the addition of advanced placement classes would remedy whatever problems were associated with public education. Further, after the *Brown* decision, any primacy of states' rights over federal law in the form of state-imposed desegregation was illegal. Although Friedman voiced his support for integration by asserting the primacy of freedom to choose over equality, Friedman's proposal would have directly or indirectly furthered segregation (Lowe and Miner 1966).

Even though Friedman's proposal was rejected by the public in a time of increased government spending, it would return with a vengeance in the late 1980s and early 1990s when Americans began to define less government with economic and social superiority. The conservative proposal for educational reform would find currency and expression in these later decades and directly give rise to the development of privatization, public choice, and charter schools as educational reform movements. The proposal would prove to be one of the biggest and most controversial issues in U.S. politics at the beginning of the twenty-first century.

The importance of the post–World War II era in education is significant for any understanding of the current debates regarding public schools and, specifically, charter schools. Issues regarding states' rights, race, market initiatives, the role of government and "failing U.S. schools," so predominant in the educational discourse of the 1950s, encompassed some of the identical topics and questions that the educational community has to deal with today. The development of the charter school reform movement must be understood as a direct outgrowth of the issues that faced the United States as a nation in the 1950s and those that continue to haunt and spawn educational debate today.

The 1960s and the Politics of Education

If the United States experienced conformity in the 1950s, the 1960s were anything but conventional. Changes in educational policy during the 1960s and issues that composed the debate over educational purpose and access must be situated and understood within the context of the political activism and resistance that marked the decade. Antiwar demonstrations, the civil rights movement, boycotts, the emergence of the gay movement in 1969, multiculturalism, feminism, assassinations of political leaders, and multiple marches on Washington, D.C., all worked directly to change the conception of the United States and the consciousness of its citizens. The decade of the 1960s was also to have a dramatic and far-reaching impact on educational issues and schooling.

Probably the most important political event of the 1960s was the passage of the Civil Rights Act in 1964. Not only did passage of the act guarantee African Americans access to all public facilities, it empowered the U.S. government to assure compliance with the act by authorizing it to bring suit against any institution or local government body that discriminated. According to estimates, almost 99 percent of black students in the eleven southern states were in segregated schools at the time the act was passed (Orfield 1969, 45), and schools that remained segregated were now to be stripped of any federal aid. The government played a direct and active role in the reconstitution of educational opportunity and access.

Another legislative enactment of consequence in the 1960s was the passage of the Elementary and Secondary Act in 1965. Signed into law by President Lyndon Johnson as part of the war on poverty, the act provided another nail in the coffin for segregated schools by bringing even more African Americans into the mainstream of public schooling.

With the fight over desegregation often being a violent one, the Supreme Court was once again forced to act when it decided in the case of *Green v. City School Board* in 1968. The issue involved so-called freedom-of-choice plans that had been adopted in some southern areas as a way of avoiding desegregation. The *Green* decision outlawed these schemes as barriers to desegregation, further assuring that schools would be desegregated in accordance with the *Brown* decision. Once again, the notion of choice was to become a major factor in the educational and political arenas.

In the late 1950s and the decade of the 1960s, there was an increasingly desegregated school system in the United States and immense changes in public education, especially in the South. For the first time, African Americans were allowed to attend public schools with whites, albeit at times under the protection of national guard troops. Universal access to education was hatched from the struggle for equality and justice on behalf of African Americans, members of labor unions, students, feminists, and other groups.

There were also intense debates over school curriculum in the 1960s. The roots of what is currently termed as "the multicultural movement" in education lie in the radical challenges put forth by progressive educational forces in the 1960s and early 1970s. The movement toward a multicultural curriculum originated largely from the country's culturally subjugated and marginalized citizens, such as African Americans, Mexican Americans, Native Americans, and women. Multicultural proponents criticized the schools for practices of discrimination in the admission of people of color; they condemned the academic establishment for its subservience to business interests; they reprimanded the schools for their racist, sexist, and culturally biased curricula; they objected to the hiring practices for women and minorities; and they exposed and condemned the practice of tracking, placing students on hierarchical tracks or levels of learning and opportunity. They lambasted the curriculum for its claim of neutrality, and they labored assiduously for the passage of beneficial entitlement programs such as bilingual education and Title VII–mandated educational programs.

Multiculturalists argued that a lack of understanding and an acceptance of racial differences were recognized problems for both teachers and students (Stent, Hazard, and Rivlin 1973, 73). From within the multicultural educational community there were calls to directly address issues of prejudice and discrimination in the classroom curricula. Multicultural theorists posited that schools should not seek to do away with cultural differences within our pluralistic society but instead should celebrate those differences in an atmosphere of educational inquiry. Therefore, they pointed out, schools should be oriented toward the cultural enrichment of all students through programs aimed at the preservation and extension of cultural pluralism. They put forth the idea that cultural diversity was a valuable resource that should be recognized, preserved, and extended, and they argued that only by directly confronting racism and prejudice could society ensure an understanding and appreciation for human dignity. Dewey's type of progressivism and DuBois's vision of education for liberation reached their apexes in the 1960s and early 1970s and threatened to reopen the debate over education and educational priorities.

The movements and educational struggles of the 1960s and early 1970s produced a new vocabulary of educational critique. Coupled with the critiques of schooling were calls for the abolition of inequality in school financing and for a commitment to federal funding for educational programs. The struggle for universal access, changes in the curriculum, and the passage of social legislation in the 1960s profoundly changed public education in the United States and gave new currency to progressive calls for a democratic educational purpose that had started with Dewey. Old progressive arguments and positions regarding the role and purposes of education that had been silenced by the cold war of the 1950s began to reemerge in the national controversy regarding education.

American identity itself was under reconsideration as diversity and an understanding and appreciation of differences became intense objects of controversy and debate, especially in universities, which at the time were sites of militancy and resistance. During the controversial years of the 1960s and early 1970s, the seeds that would eventually develop into the charter school reform movement were sown. Postmodernism, with its emphasis on difference, decentralization, devolution, and identity politics, would begin to affect the way Americans thought about education, what they expected from it, and how they would choose to organize, fund, and support it.

Conservatism, the 1980s, and the Politics of Public Education

In the 1970s, the National Education Association (NEA), the nation's largest teachers' union, endorsed a candidate for president of the

United States for the first time. Jimmy Carter received the endorsement of this union in his bid for the presidency in 1976 mainly because of his expressed intent to establish a cabinet-level Department of Education. The NEA had lobbied for such a national cabinet position since World War I, and with the union's endorsement, Carter was finally able to raise education to the cabinet level in 1979.

Although Carter proved to be more conservative than many observers had expected from an "education president," there is little doubt that Ronald Reagan, Carter's successor, left a lasting conservative ideological stamp on public education in the United States. Considering the Department of Education an unnecessary expense and perceiving of it as opposed to states' rights, Reagan sought to abolish the department directly after he took office in 1981. Invoking the rhetoric of free market enterprise and the logic of market-driven forces as the panacea to the country's social and economic troubles, Reagan and his administration embarked on restructuring social policy, including education, to reflect the primacy of market solutions to public problems (Lugg 1996). Education became part and parcel of a larger debate over the role of government, regulations, and free market capitalism.

Calls for the elimination of the Department of Education met with severe resistance by progressive and liberal educators, which made it impossible for the conservatives to abolish the department. As a result, the Reagan administration sought to reconstitute the Department of Education, transforming it into a vocal advocate for controversial policies like organized prayer, public and private school choice, and school vouchers. As a result, blistering attacks were increasingly leveled against public education, teachers' unions, and curriculum. The department began to actively work against the interests of the educational stakeholders in the public schools.

In 1983, the best-publicized educational achievement of the Reagan administration was issued in the form of a book-length report entitled *A Nation at Risk*. Issued by the National Commission on Excellence in Education (NCEE), the report provided a scathing critique of the public education system, arguing that U.S. education had become a bastion of mediocrity. The report concluded that the state of education in the United States was actually threatening the nation's future economic growth. With its dire predictions and warnings, *A Nation at Risk* once again focused public attention on the issue of education as an economic issue, and as educational urgency took on market proportions, progressive educational concerns were not considered a priority. The controversy regarding improvement in U.S. education was now firmly attached to the perceived need to link the country's readiness to educational standards and school performance. And this aim was to be best accomplished, in the eyes of conservative politicians and their constituencies, in a free and unbridled marketplace. The failure of public education and "government schools" became favorite topics for those who proposed market solutions to educational problems.

After *A Nation at Risk* was released in 1983, scores of magazines and news reports jumped on the bandwagon and concentrated on the supposed "failure of public education." For instance, *Newsweek* rushed a scathing story to press asking if the schools could be saved, and the sum of the report was that progress from generation to generation was being "shattered" by the mediocre condition of the U.S. schools ("Saving Our Schools" 1983).

Responsibility for the economic recession that plagued the United States during the early 1980s was placed squarely on the public educational system. Public education was no longer cast as an expression and vehicle for economic excellence and national security but was looked at as inhibiting economic growth (Shor 1986, 108). Like the *Sputnik* scare decades earlier, *A Nation at Risk* sounded a wake-up call to educators and policymakers, but this time the call was, not for an improved public educational system, but for a private one. This time, instead of Soviet superiority in outer space, it was the influx of quality goods from Japan that was to be considered the threat to national security. It was argued that the ability of the United States to compete globally was being jeopardized by a public educational system that simply did not work. Proponents of privatization and free-market solutions to educational crises began to emerge with think tanks and funding that had not existed before.

To build the case for a mediocre school system, the NCEE turned to an analysis of Scholastic Aptitude Test (SAT) scores to make its point. The NCEE pointed to the long SAT score decline from 1963 to 1980, and it also began to publicly compare U.S. education to other Western school systems. Playing to a sense of political patriotism and economic nationalism, *A Nation at Risk* pointed out that the United States would continue to be a preeminent country only so long as material benefits and great ideas remained a part of the country's legacy and argued that the nation's national security was in jeopardy as long as public schools threatened this legacy.

In June 1983, another report, entitled *Action for Excellence: A Comprehensive Plan to Improve our Nation's Schools,* was published by a state governors' group called the Education Commission of the States (ECS). Often referred to as the Hunt Report, after Governor James B. Hunt of North Carolina, this report continued to echo the notion that U.S. schools were failing (Education Commission of the States 1983, 3).

The alarms did not stop with the Hunt Report. The next major statement regarding the state of public education was issued in September 1983 in a National Science Board (NSB) report. In its dramatic work *Educating Americans for the 21st Century,* the NSB warned that

> the nation that dramatically and boldly led the world into the age of technology is failing to provide its own children with the intellectual tools needed for the 21st century. . . . Already the quality of our manufactured products, the viability of our trade, our leadership in research and development, our standard of living, are strongly challenged. Our children could be stragglers in a world of technology. We must not let this happen; America must not become an industrial dinosaur. We must not provide our children a 1960's education for the 21st century world. (National Science Board 1983, 9)

The exigencies of education were once again being linked to the nation's economic readiness, or lack of it.

In the 1980s, not only was the public's obsession with everything private fueled but the case for a *super*functionalism was built. Instead of the rudimentary skills required by the social functionalism during the time of industrialization, the new information and technological revolution that was taking place needed a different type of worker with different kinds of skills. Preparing students for the twenty-first century's technological and cybernetic revolution, or "the third wave," became the mantra of reports similar to *A Nation at Risk.* Calls to focus education on "back to basics" became the antidote for the economic crisis, similar to the "objectives first" clamor in the early 1900s. The NSB defined the new cognitive-economic relationship between school and work as follows:

> Alarming numbers of young Americans are ill-equipped to work in, to contribute to, profit from and enjoy our increasingly technological society. Far too many emerge from the nation's elementary and secondary schools with an inadequate grounding in mathematics, science, and technology. This situation must not continue. . . . We must return to the basics, but the "basics" of the 21st century are not only reading, writing, and arithmetic. They include communication, and higher problem-solving skills, and scientific and technological literacy. (National Science Board 1983, 12)

The superfunctionalism and new basics, now defined as "ultra-basics," included science, computers, higher-order reasoning, social studies, foreign languages, and correct use of English. What were once thought to be basic skills were now obsolete, and schools were now to place the ultrabasics at the core of their curriculum. While "the second wave" of educational restructuring was established for the industrial age of the 1900s, "the third wave" restructuring movement of the 1980s focused on preparing students for the information/technology age.

The educator Larry Hutchins expressed the new third-wave superfunctionalist restructuring argument like this: "The old design [schools] worked relatively well for the society it served; it brought schooling to millions of immigrants [who] . . . were needed to stoke the engines of the industrial society. Today's society no longer requires such a work force. We need people who can think and solve problems using information and technology" (Hutchins 1990, 1).

Maintaining the U.S. "empire," creating better goods and services, dominating world markets under the guise of competition, and creating the new workforce of the future were all interwoven into the calls for a new and radical restructuring of schools. Any discussions as to what type of society Americans wished to create or the relationships among school, democracy, culture, and the emerging cybernetic society were conspicuously absent from these discussions. Furthermore, much like the efficiency-of-production arguments of the industrial age, teachers were encouraged to develop curricular goals based on step-by-step procedures and time schedules that corresponded to "the schools of tomorrow" (Goodman 1995, 10). The superfunctionalism was now itself a business, offering teachers corporate educational solutions in the form of kits, packages, services, and products.

During the 1980s, the educational reform movement once again increasingly found expression in a language of business efficiency, productivity, and the application of management theories to the educational enterprise. More than at any other time, test scores became the products of the schools. Students became the workers who created this product using instructional programs given to them by "the educational organization." Teachers were transformed into shop managers who presided over the students' production; school principals became the plant managers who managed the school personnel; and specialists, such as social workers or school counselors, were employed to handle the students' emotional needs (Goodman 1995, 11).

Transformed into being classroom managers overseeing the student-workers, teachers became further disengaged and divorced from the nature of teaching as they were galvanized to follow prescribed "teaching recipes" in the form of corporate produced, preformulated lesson plans. With the increasing rise of prepackaged instructional materials in the 1980s, intellectual engagement with the curriculum had now become for many teachers a luxury, as they were transformed into mere managers of learning in service to the state tests. For many of these teachers, charter schools offered a way to escape these educational prescriptions for learning and to reconceive of education as an act of creativity rather than one of constraint. For many teachers, charter schools were a way out of a depersonalized system and offered the hope of developing personalized learning, innovative teaching, and deeper and more meaningful associations.

SCHOOL CHOICE AND THE POLITICS OF THE CHARTER MOVEMENT IN THE 1990s

The development of the new educational discourse of business productivity and efficiency in the 1980s set the stage for the current educational controversies at the beginning of the second millenium. As the United States exited the 1980s, unregulated capitalist markets and corporate globalization monopolized mainstream thinking and created a psychology of privatization. Determined that market-driven solutions offered the remedy to all social problems, private or public, economists and pundits warned that the United States should concentrate on market solutions to human problems if it were to compete vigorously in the global arena. Unregulated markets and privatization were seen as an advantage for all those interested in the notion of American progress and institutional reform.

With the fall of the Soviet Union in 1991, this vision of the United States, a country with unregulated markets and a capitalist hegemony, became the primary vision for education as well. Not only were public schools continually perceived as failing and mediocre, the argument now began to pose the possibility that these public schools would better serve the country's citizens if they were forced to compete with schools that were privatized. As the argument went, schools need to develop students the way corporations develop products. School choice proponents now claimed that the government should provide vouchers to pay for the schooling students or their parents wished them to have. The idea, claimed voucher adherents, was that private and public schools could then compete for the most academically able students. The schools that did not prepare students for the emerging information/technology-driven market in an efficient manner would lose out to a "natural selection" (Kincheloe 2000, 171). Friedman's forty-year-old proposal for privatized education had now found a suitable political environment and developed into a fait accompli.

For the first time in a real way, the notion of public education itself was being questioned by a new generation of super-, social functionalists and private market economists. And while the majority of educational discussions and debates in the past had focused on how to bring the country's public school system up to speed, the new superfunctionalist arguments actually questioned the very efficacy, existence, and necessity of public schools. Education was now being conceived of as an "educational marketplace," and a new language of "choice" began to emerge to define the terms of the debate. Progressive educational concerns regarding the role of democracy, equity, and social justice were purged from educational discourse in favor, once more, of competitiveness, efficiency, and productivity needs. The new rhetoric of privatized schooling and "choice" defined the terms of the debate, and Americans, in a very real way, were now embroiled in a controversy over the continued existence of public education itself.

The charter school proposal in many ways is a turning point in educational discourse. Charter schools bring up issues of individual choice and actually question whether the nation can really hope to achieve, or any longer even want, a common public school experience. Yet, just as charter schools offer new challenges and possibilities, they reflect the evolutionary compilation of historical arguments and disagreements over the nature of American schools, what they are supposed to accomplish, how they will be organized, who they will serve, and what they will teach. The entire notion of modernism and the factory school is now being called into question. The current reality seems to favor decentralization and challenge large public institutions that claim to universally serve all citizens.

The Politics of School Choice

During the 1980s, the whole idea of school choice in the United States was associated with free markets and individualism. Many political and educational policymakers insisted that the government should exist only to guarantee and preserve individual liberty. Motivated by the belief that public education was antithetical to the public interest and that a free market was the best way to organize education for all the nation's citizens, many conservatives embraced private choice as a way of dismantling public education in its entirety (Rinehart and Lee 1991). The private choice argument that had not caught the public's attention in the 1950s now found an audience in a shifting political environment in which the people had lost confidence in anything public, including public education. Private choice was now a major policy issue for schools.

The strongest academic voices for private choice in education have been John Chubb and Terry Moe. In their book *Politics, Markets, and American Schools,* Chubb and Moe devoted their analysis to demonstrating that private choice would enhance student achievement. Published by the Brookings Institute in 1990, their book helped to move the argument for private choice and educational vouchers out of the conservative camp and into the mainstream. More important, the book was the first attempt to ground support for privatized choice in scholarly terms (Chubb and Moe 1990).

Chubb and Moe's analysis went so far as to argue that private choice itself "has the capacity all by itself to bring about the kind of transformation that, for years, reforms have been seeking to engineer in a myriad of ways" (Chubb and Moe 1990, 217). According to these two authors, allowing parents and educational consumers to have a "choice" in the kind of school they want their children to attend would fix what is wrong with U.S. education by providing competition. It would also give those parents better resources to find an educational marketplace in which "the human capital" of their children could be developed at higher levels. Chubb and Moe's argument, then, reasoned that public schools should be forced to compete with private schools for tax dollars. Not only should parents have the right to choose, they argued, it was choice itself that would fix the schools. The answer was the Friedman proposal of 1955: allow parents to receive a voucher they could use to buy a quality education for their children. For Chubb and Moe, the argument was simple: students, not schools, should receive public funds in the form of vouchers.

The underlying assumption behind the private voucher proposal is the claim that allowing parents the freedom to act as rational educational consumers with the ability to take their business elsewhere if dissatisfied with the level of education their children are receiving will force all schools to increase their efficiency. Schools that do not, private choice claimants argue, will risk extinction.

Market advocates for school reform maintain that students are consumers of education as a product, much like they are of athletic shoes or designer clothing. According to voucher advocates, education needs to be treated as a purchase that parents and their children make in the educational marketplace. Only by reducing education to individual choice, maintain private choice advocates, can meaningful educational reform take place.

The Emergence of Public Choice

The controversy over choice took distinct and particular forms as the 1990s progressed. In many ways, public choice arose as a concept as an attempt to head off the movement for the privatization of schools through private vouchers. But in a significant way, the call for public choice also reflected changing global political and socioeconomic realities.

Public choice is part of a historical evolution: an evolution from modernism, characterized in the United States by the rise of industrialism, to postmodernism, or the developing cybernetic revolution in information and technology. As production and consumption are being redefined by the advent of the computer and post–assembly-line approaches to work, the notion of a national identity as one single identity is currently being questioned. Diversity is now a secure part of the country's ideological character—and cultural differences, class differences, ethnic differences, and ideological, religious, and philosophical differences are now leading many people to question the entire notion of a universal system of public education. And with rapid changes in consumption and production, the factory-school model of education is being called into question as it pertains to new levels of human development—both technological and social.

The modern epoch of education, the historical period between the Renaissance and the late twentieth century, occurred during a shifting emphasis from an agrarian society to an industrial society. Although modernity was synonymous with industrialization and the shift from the first wave (agrarian production) to the second wave (industrial production), the current socioeconomic and political global reality is characterized by rapid cybernetic changes in the way Americans and the people in other societies now produce and consume. Postmodernism now represents a shift from the second wave (industrialism) to the third wave (cybernetic/technological revolution). Throughout the world, these changes have sparked what appear to be new controversies over the challenges that face schools, and the result has been an emphasis on school choice in hundreds of countries throughout the world, not just the United States (Whitty, Power, and Halpin 1998).

Public school choice promises to be many things to many different people, and it therefore represents a very complex and unique educational reform movement—one that must be analyzed and understood as a "moving mosaic" (Hargreaves 1994). Even though different groups that support charter schools may experience intense dissatisfaction with the state-run educational process, they also have very different reasons for their frustration and dissatisfaction.

For many diverse groups and for many different reasons, the charter school idea, or public school choice, offers distinct advantages. Furthermore, many parents, teachers, students, and educational policymakers who support public school choice and the charter movement do so with a heavy commitment to public schools in general. They look at public school choice, and specifically charter schools, as a way to strengthen the nation's commitment to public education. They are against privatized choice, which they believe is an attack on public schools, but are in favor of public choice as a reform measure for restructuring schools.

Deborah Meier, educational reformer and founder of the Central Park East Elementary School in New York City, explained the important distinction between privatized choice and public choice this way:

> There are two unrelated perspectives, and they both use the word choice. When many conservatives talk about choice, they mean that private enterprise and the marketplace are better and that public institutions are, by their very nature, inferior. We need to dismiss the idea that the concept of choice has anything to do with such proposals. They are not about choice at all. They are about privatization and a means to get rid of public education. . . . When I have argued for choice, it has had nothing to do with abandoning public education. It has been a way to argue against the factory model of education. (Meier 1996, 101)

For many public choice advocates, charter schools can be enthusiastically welcomed precisely because they appear to promise to protect public education as an institution while at the same time provide opportunities for fundamental restructuring and reform. And because the vast majority of U.S. students will continue to attend public schools, the argument goes, they should have the same kind of choice that students in private schools enjoy (Young and Clinchy 1992).

Competition and Public School Choice

Whether choice is looked at as an opportunity or as a disaster, the most commonly held rationale behind the choice argument, public or private, is that competition provides the best or most efficient motor for change. The premise of the contention is similar to the private voucher argument, that schools can be best improved by competitive market mechanisms. Like private choice, the public choice rationale maintains that schools and student learning improve when public schools have to compete for students and that students and their parents have the right to choose. According to its staunchest advocates, public school choice is simply about one particular charter school or another as much as it is about raising the educational standards of all public schools.

Ted Kolderie, a leading charter school adherent, has stated the goals of competition this way: "For those who enact the laws it is to create dynamics that will cause the mainline district system (school) to change and to improve. The charter schools, helpful as they may be to the students who enroll in them, are instrumental" (Kolderie 1998, 4).

The Hudson Institute agreed, noting that "the whole point of charter schools is to answer today's call for bold school reform by injecting freedom, choice and accountability into school systems and thereby providing a better education for America's children" (Vanourek et al. 1997, 23). Joe Nathan, a charter school advocate and organizer, echoes similar sentiments:

> The charter idea is not just about the creation of new, more accountable public schools or the conversion of existing public schools. The charter idea also introduces fair, thoughtful competition into public education. Strong charter laws allow these schools to be sponsored by more than one type of public organization, for example, a local school board, a state school board, or a public university. Evidence shared later shows that when school districts know families can get a public education from more than one source, that competition helps produce improvements. (Nathan 1999, xxviii)

Yet not all public policymakers and educational theoreticians would agree. Some educational policymakers argue that competition through choice, whether it is public or private, undermines a shared citizenship in U.S. society and is little more than a slippery slope to individualized, privatized education. The lack of a common educational leadership, these opponents maintain, helps ensure that the argument for charter schools is dominated, not by educational ideas, but by economic necessity (Molnar 1996, 5). Protesting against competition and in favor of cooperation, these educators claim that the concept of choice threatens the community and shared citizenship necessary for the realization of democracy and democratic citizenship. Asserting that competitive, individual choice supplants shared decision making, educational policy groups such as the Carnegie Foundation for the Advancement of Teaching reason that the Darwinian market mechanism of choice used to weed out the weakest schools in fact exacerbates inequities among districts (Carnegie Foundation for the Advancement of Teaching 1992). It does so, claim opponents, because when students move out of their district to one charter school or another, they take the funding from their own district with them. If the new district has a higher per-pupil cost, the move means that the home district, which is often already suffering from low funding, pays far more to educate the transfer students, which leaves even less for those that remain behind. The districts that begin with fewer resources are left with even fewer with which to educate their own students.

Recently, Howard Koenig, a superintendent of schools in Roosevelt, New York, expressed the concern that charter schools in the state of New York will drain off millions from their districts and will lead to tax hikes and program cost increases. He and other superintendents have joined with some parents and unions to oppose charter school legislation. Les Black, superintendent of Brentwood schools in New York state, estimated his district has lost $1 million as a result of New York charter schools that have recently been approved. According to Black, "There's precious little research on charter schools" (Pratt 2000). Thus, the Carnegie Foundation argues, "If fair competition is to occur, all states with 'choice' programs must first resolve the financial disparities that exist from district to district" (Pratt 2000, 20).

And, of course, the argument brings up the question of school funding in its entirety: how schools are subsidized and whether we want to continue the practice of funding our public schools mainly through local property taxes. Many politicians and educational policymakers argue that the chances that the market and competition will create educational opportunities and options for all parents are limited by the current financing mechanisms employed to subsidize the public schools. And, they maintain, without equity in funding, charter schools will do little to correct the state of education in the United States. They also claim that if freeing the charter schools from burdensome regulation and reams of legal considerations works, then why are these same freedoms not offered to the traditional public schools? How can public schools compete, they ask, if they must continue to operate under regulations and restrictions that the charter schools can simply avoid?

The issue of educational equity is paramount to numerous educational interests, and certain policymakers see public school choice as a way to accelerate what is already an inequitable situation. In a study of small, private Catholic schools, Anthony Bryk and Valerie Lee noted:

> Market forces, for example, cannot explain the broadly shared institutional purpose of advancing social equity. Nor can they account for the efforts of Catholic educators to maintain inner-city schools (with large non-Catholic enrollments) while facing mounting fiscal woes. Likewise, market forces cannot easily explain why resources are allocated within schools in a compensatory fashion in order to provide an academic education for every student. Nor can they explain the norms of community that infuse daily life in these schools. (Bryk and Lee 1993, 11)

For educators like Bryk and Lee, the answer to providing quality education lies with developing a higher notion of community, not simply pursuing naked self-interests through competitive choice. They also argue that the communal effects they noted in the Catholic schools they used as the object of their study were the result of face-to-face contacts and a sense of sharing and caring between teachers and students. They also claim that this communal experience is a result of a moral authority that results in a "set of shared beliefs about what students should learn, the development of proper norms of instruction, and how people should relate to one another" (Bryk and Lee 1993, 7).

Bryk and Lee's admonitions regarding the market's claim to provide quality community education through choice strike a chord with many other educational policymakers who are opposed to charter schools. The claim that the notion of public choice is built on the idea that society can be held together solely by the self-interested pursuits of individual actors in the educational arena is not palatable to many educational interests.

One leading opponent of charter schools and privatization, Jonathan Kozol, a Pulitzer Prize–winning educational author, argues that charter schools only isolate the privileged elite (Manetto 1999). For opponents like Kozol, the charter school idea, and public choice itself, represents a contemporary, postmodern rejection of the possibility of a common school for all citizens. As a result, they argue, the idea threatens to turn the relationship between society and its educational needs into little more than a commercial transaction based on individual self-interests and competitive self-advantage.

Charter School Supporters

An interesting aspect of the current debate regarding charter schools is the variety of philosophies and positions that support the concept. The contemporary discussion about charter schools is unlike the earlier debates that marked the beginning of the twentieth century, debates in which progressive educators and social functionalists found themselves on opposite sides of the controversy. With charter schools, the issue is far more complex, and its acceptance as an idea among a wide range of educational interests and communities is far more diverse.

Many progressive educators, in the tradition of Dewey, DuBois, and others, support charter schools, and they do so for several reasons. To begin with, they question modernity itself, especially its emphasis on scientific and technical bureaucratic rationality. This questioning translates into curricular concerns about such issues as student-centered classrooms and logistical concerns such as length of the school day and how students learn and study. And as previously mentioned, some people look to public choice and charter schools as a method of discouraging total privatization of schools—reasoning that allowing public choice will prevent the wholesale loss of public schools (Young and Clinchy 1992). Others, such as the educator Deborah Meier, look to the charter idea as a method of creating community schools that can experiment with creativity and innovation.

For many progressive educators, like Meier, charter schools offer an opportunity to break down factory schools and the factory style of education. The postmodern situation in this country's society leads to an opportunity to create small, intimate schools and communities that organize their philosophies around curricula and teaching methods that encourage self-reflection and democratic citizenship. Breaking with the factory model of education completely, something that was never realized during the modernism of Dewey's time, can now become a postmodern reality, and this fact, educators like Meier argue, will serve to raise the educational efficacy of all public schools.

Meier, like other progressives who support charter schools, presumes that public schools can be strengthened, not weakened, with the option of public choice. In her book *The Power of Their Ideas,* Meier makes a passionate plea for preserving and strengthening public education. She is also critical of many progressive educators who have dismissed public school choice:

> Progressive policy makers and legislators have on the whole allowed their concern with equity to lead them to reflexively attack choice as inherently elitist (naturally, choice doesn't tend to make friends among educational bureaucrats either). This is, I believe, a grave mistake. The argument over choice, unlike the one over private school vouchers, offers progressives an opportunity. After all, it wasn't so long ago that progressive educators were enthusiastically supporting schools of choice, usually called alternative schools. These alternatives were always on the fringe, as though the vast majority of schools were doing just fine. We now have a chance to make such alternatives the mainstream, not just for avant-garde "misfits" or "nerds" or "those more at risk." (Meier 1995, 92–93)

Meier and her supporters insist that successful experiments in public education—innovation and creativity—are the result of expanded choices and the diversity in experimentation that public choice brings. The factory-style school that dominates U.S. education, they argue, is not inevitable but historical, and public choice allows for new and innovative challenges to this concept. Further, Meier displays her exasperation with people who dismiss public choice by noting that many concerned policymakers and progressives who are dead set against choice because of its impact on equity are already exercising choice for their own children. While arguing against public choice, these progressives are either sending their children to private schools, moving to more-affluent communities where the schools tend to be better, taking whatever necessary means they need to take to make sure that their children qualify for gifted programs, or selecting specialized schools (Meier 1995, 99). According to Meier, "What we must do is shape the concept of choice into a consciously equitable instrument for restructuring public education so that over time all parents can have the kinds of choices the favored few now have, but in ways that serve rather than undercut public goals" (Meier 1995, 99).

Deborah Meier is not alone in embracing public school choice. Many other progressive educational policymakers find that public school choice offers the educational community, parents, teachers, administrators, students, and community members the chance to achieve greater parental and community control over schools. In some inner cities, charter schools have had tremendous neighborhood involvement and appear to have been a source of revitalized community participation in local schools (Rofes 1996, 50–51).

Many parents and teachers support charter schools because of curriculum concerns. Some members of minority communities argue that traditional schools are focused on narrow conceptions of valued knowledge based on Eurocentric notions of intelligence, and certain educators claim that teachers fail to match their instruction to the cultural backgrounds of their students. They criticize many educational practices for failing to offer multicultural experiences to students, and, as a result, they argue, marginalized groups, such as African Americans, often must work with a curriculum that fails to reflect their lives, values, needs, and cultural distinctions (Tyack 1993). For many low-income and minority families, charter schools offer a way to legitimize their knowledge and celebrate their cultural backgrounds by developing curricula around cultural and/or ethnic identity.

Many charter school advocates promote centricity in their curriculum goals, such as Afro-centricity or Mexican-centricity. They want their students to have a greater knowledge and appreciation of their cultural history. The movement to begin charter schools is a uniquely postmodern movement and involves fighting for independence from what they believe to be a state-controlled system of oppression (Wells et al. 1999).

Home-schooling advocates of all persuasions also favor the notion of public choice and charter schools because charter schools enable them to withdraw from the public school system; educate their children at home according to whatever philosophical, pedagogical, or religious orientation they wish; and still receive public funding. They are not asked to adopt one method of instruction, and therefore each family can make its own pedagogical decisions as to what is valued knowledge and what culture it wishes to reflect in the curriculum. And although home-schooling families are held accountable to state educational standards, they can emphasize particular philosophies within a like-minded community (Wells et al. 1999, 13). Thus, home-schooling charters can range from fundamental Christian families to secular humanist families. Charters also allow older students, who for whatever reason have dropped out of regular public schools, to finish their schooling at home through independent study programs. These students can earn true high school degrees as opposed to general equivalency diplomas.

Opposition to Public Choice and the Charter School Movement

Some educators are adamantly against any consideration of public school choice, be it for a charter school or otherwise, arguing that charter schools represent a slippery slope to the eventual disinvestment of public schools and the destruction of the idea of a common school (Molnar 1996, 5). These educators also worry that public choice is really a step toward privatizing education through vouchers, not a way of preventing it.

They concede that the charter movement may free some marginalized groups and citizens to start their own schools based on new and innovative curricula and ideas, but they contend that charters will do little or nothing at all to address the material inequalities that are expanding throughout the world. They contend that charter schools will simply create educationally excellent enclaves, not better public educational systems. By failing to consider larger postmodern socioeconomic issues implicated in the institutional life of societies, many educators argue that charter schools cannot deliver the emancipatory promise they offer and, in fact, will end up simply reproducing the inequalities that are expanding in what they see as a new postindustrial, global society (Whitty, Power, and Halpin 1998). They claim that within the context of inequitable and institutionalized sociopolitical relations, charter schools can do little to offer real educational reform.

The Controversy over For-Profit Management Firms

One of the main concerns that numerous educators from all political persuasions have centers on the for-profit management firms, like the Edison Project and Educational Alternatives Incorporated (EAI), which have been some of the most visible and vocal backers of charter schools. Such firms are allowed to manage charter schools and currently are operating in Boston, Michigan, and other states (Whitty, Power, and Halpin 1998, 48). The greatest concern that opponents to these management firms express is that the for-profit companies will use charter schools as a way to accelerate privatization in public education. They maintain that such companies are more interested in profit than in improving education.

The growth of for-profit companies to run publicly funded schools, such as charter schools, has exploded. Since 1997, more than a dozen firms have sprung up to manage and operate charter schools, and as of the year 2000, for-profit management firms are responsible for teaching some 100,000 students at about 200 schools throughout the country. Boston-based Advantage Schools shot from $4 million in revenues to $60 million in four years, and Edison Project Incorporated jumped from $12 million to $217 million in revenues in just five years. Edison now runs seventy-nine schools in sixteen states ("For Profit Schools" 2000).

Advocates of privately managed public schools have an even greater vision for the future. Edison plans to manage 423 schools by the year 2005, with 260,000 students and revenues of $1.8 billion. And that is just the beginning. Big name investors, such as J. P. Morgan and Fidelity Investments, are gearing up for large investments in private school management ("For Profit Schools" 2000, 64).

In North Lauderdale, Florida, Charter Schools USA has received $110,000 for feasibility studies and the development of a North Lauderdale charter application. For managing the school, Charter Schools USA's annual fee will be 10 percent of the school's operating budget, which is expected to be about $1.5 million in the first year. The budget is expected to increase to $3.3 million by the end of the third year, after grades eleven and twelve have been added. According to Jonathan Hage, a former conservative analyst at the Heritage Foundation and founder of Charter Schools USA: "This is the most unbelievable business in the world. We're in the first stages of privatizing education" ("Charter Schools" 1998, 1).

Companies like Advantage and the Edison Project pledge to have most students doing college level work by the eleventh grade, and they tie the curriculum directly to standards and standardized testing. Much like the social functionalists of the early 1900s, these companies embrace the notion of superfunctionalism, promising to raise test scores and competitively prepare students for the information/technologically based workplace. Yet according to Ann Bastian, senior program officer at the New World Foundation, an educational think tank and advocacy group:

> We have the right to be skeptical about good intentions when the bottom line is profitability not education. These educational entrepreneurs have attracted high-profile educators and contracts, but they have not been able to stay the course. They often promise to bring new resources to a school district, but in practice they are front loading their programs with technology, new teachers, and a fresh coat of paint. They have diverted resources from other public school programs, and from their investors. But they have not made schools work better over time, nor helped other schools improve, nor taken on the challenge of system-wide change, nor contributed to solving the enormous problem of school finance. (Bastian 1996, 48)

In fact, the companies have been less than profitable. Edison lost $49 million with a revenue of $133 million in 1999, and its stock has slumped nearly 25 percent since its initial public offering in November 1999. On 3 January 2000, the Tesseract Group Incorporated, formerly Education Alternatives Incorporated, said that the NASDAQ stock exchange was threatening to delist its shares. The company, as of March 2000, was trading for less than a dollar a share ("For Profit Schools" 2000, 65).

Numerous educators, like Bastian, maintain that if companies show that schools can work if they are given adequate resources like technology, then the real issue becomes, not the companies themselves, but how to ensure that funding exists for all schools, not just a select few. They also maintain that the for-profit companies do nothing to confront the fundamental problem of school financing.

Charter school opponents are critical of the for-profit management relationship between private management companies and public schools for ideological reasons as well. They claim that the arrangement is a wholesale subsidization of private profit through public funds, and they argue that the for-profit companies are actually cutting essential services and extracurricular activities in the charter schools they operate. For example, few of the company-managed schools offer a school lunch program or transportation for students who live in outlying towns. Extracurricular programs, such as some sports programs, are limited. Also, most schools run by for-profit companies are not equipped to handle special education students. According to Secretary of Education Richard W. Riley, "It is a lot more expensive to educate a child who is disabled or emotionally troubled" ("For Profit Schools" 2000, 65). The bottom line for the for-profit firms consists of money and profits for shareholders. Cost consciousness, the focus of these companies, requires that they cut what they consider to be "frivolous" programs.

Opponents of for-profit public charter schools also argue that when knowledge is reduced to a commodity, in essence something that is bartered for and sold in the marketplace, learning itself is reduced to the mere act of producing a product. Innumerable people in the education establishment argue that the goals of public education will be compromised if education is reduced primarily to profit motives and shareholder interests. And, they maintain, much as progressives like Dewey did, that slavish allegiance to standards and standardized tests will reduce education to an act of consuming, not producing and learning.

The Controversy over the Segregation of Schools

Other progressive educators are concerned that charter schools, or public choice, could lead to the resegregation of schools through unfair and discriminatory admission policies (Cobb and Glass 1999). They claim that charter schools further stratify schools on the basis of race, class, and socioeconomic status (Corwin and Flaherty 1995). For example, in one urban district in California, educators and Latino parents struggled successfully to form a school that catered to the Latino students' cultural history and origins. In doing so, they ended up separating themselves politically and socially from African Americans and other racial groups in the school district (Wells et al. 1999, 20).

In a study of ethnic and class stratification in fifty-five urban and fifty-seven rural charter schools in Arizona done for Education Policy Analysis, a nonprofit think tank, researchers noted that nearly half the charter schools studied exhibited evidence of substantial ethnic separation (Cobb and Glass 1999, 1). They concluded that subtle exclusionary practices among charter schools, including initial parent contacts and the provision of transportation, had an appreciable effect on ethnic and racial segregation in charter schools:

> The ethnic separation on the part of Arizona's charter schools, though de facto, is an insidious by-product of unregulated school choice. If parents can choose where to send their children to school, they are

likely to choose schools with students of similar orientations to their own. Moreover, it is well documented that chooses (in this case, charter students and parents) differ from nonchooses in several meaningful ways, which further contributes to the stratification of students along ethnic and socioeconomic lines. (Cobb and Glass 1999, 1)

In North Carolina, when the state legislators were debating charter schools, it was feared there would be a recurrence of the flight of white academies that had been a historical part of the South a generation earlier in the aftermath of the *Brown* decision. In approving the charter idea, the legislators put a clause in the legislation that required the schools to reasonably reflect the demographics of the school districts they serve. Yet two years after passage of the legislation, twenty-two of the state's charter schools appeared to violate the diversity clause (Dent 1998). The irony lies in the fact that the law is being violated by charter schools that are 85 percent black and populated by children whose parents sought to flee the failing public schools.

The charter school movement is having the effect of resegregating schools in North Carolina, and thus it poses a legal and social dilemma. Many policymakers are asking how, if the charter school movement is really going to be a public choice reform, can that be accomplished without resegregating the schools? Or can it? And where charter schools are located in predominantly black neighborhoods, how can they be centers for diversity if few white parents want to send their children to those schools?

Racial and ethnic segregation and stratification can happen subtly: in the way the schools are organized, how they state their mission, and the symbols and signifiers they use to attract students. For example, in a suburban charter school in California, the founders created a high-tech image and orientation for the school. This emphasis permitted marketing strategies to attract students whose parents worked in the technology industry, which, in turn, resulted in the procurement of more computers and software for the school through grants and donations. Creating an ideological mission for the school along with the symbols of technology and computer literacy meant that this charter school could subtly give the message of who belongs at the school—who will fit in and who will not (Wells et al. 1999, 22).

Not all evidence points to the fact that school districts are improving as a result of the advent of charter schools. For example, educator and charter school expert Eric Rofes, in congressional testimony before the U.S. Senate Committee on Labor and Human Resources, presented his research and findings regarding the impact of charter schools on school districts. His findings suggested that charter schools do impact on traditional school districts and that districts experienced:

1. A loss of students and often an accompanying loss of financing
2. The loss of a particular kind of student to niche-focused charter schools
3. The departure of significant numbers of disgruntled parents
4. Shifts in staff morale
5. The redistribution of some central office administrators' time and increased challenges to predicting student enrollment and planning grade levels. (U.S. Senate 1998, 7)

Rofe's study also concluded that of the twenty-five schools examined throughout the United States, in terms of responding to the advent of a charter in their district, school districts typically did not respond quickly with any dramatic improvements. His study concluded that the majority of districts that were impacted by the beginning of a charter school went about their business as usual and responded to the charter initiatives slowly, if at all. Only one-quarter of the districts responded to the charter schools with new educational programs (U.S. Senate 1998, 7). Rofe concluded with a recommendation to the Senate committee that policymakers actually create charter laws with the intent of having districts transfer new and innovative pedagogical practices to the schools in the district so that these schools do not simply become innovative havens for a select few (U.S. Senate 1998, 9).

Admission Practices and Discrimination

Opponents of charter schools are also concerned about admission practices that exclude "undesirable" or "special education" students and parents through "creaming" (Lopez, Wells, and Holme 1998). A 1999 Michigan State University study regarding charter schools in that state found that Michigan charter schools were taking students who comprised the cream of the crop financially. The report also stated that the charter schools were generally taking the students who were the cheapest to educate and leaving behind the students who cost more to educate. For example, because junior high and high school students cost more to educate owing to the need for athletic equipment, laboratories, extensive libraries, and specialized teachers, most of the groups who have opened charter schools in Michigan have elected to open elementary schools ("Michigan Charter Schools," 1999–2000).

The study also found that three-quarters of the charter schools in the state had no special education services, and even the few that did enroll special needs students provided them with fewer and less costly services than the nearby public schools did. Several early studies of charter schools have identified special education as one of the key challenges facing charter schools in the future (Urahn and Stewart 1994).

In 1995, the U.S. General Accounting Office studied charter schools in eleven states and identified a number of challenges charter schools encountered in implementing federal programs such as the Individuals with Disabilities Education Act of 1990. This study found, in particular, that because the local school district is the usual point of federal program administration, the lack of connection between some charter schools and a local district raises concern about the flow of federal money and oversight and accountability (U.S. General Accounting Office 1995).

A fairly recent Michigan State University study points out that when charter schools enroll low-cost students and exclude high-cost students, they increase the average costs for the public school districts that must provide the more expensive services (Lewin 1999). This situation threatens to impact greatly on public schools in states such as California where charter schools are allowed to select their students and can require parents to contribute resources. In such states, most charter schools are located in suburbs or small towns and enroll fewer poor and minority students than do neighboring districts. Yet a December 1999 report issued from the U.S. Department of Education's Joint Committee on Public Schools rebuts this criticism and contention. The report concluded that no "creaming" had occurred (U.S. Department of Education 1999).

Undecided Educators and Unanswered Questions

Many educators are simply undecided about charter schools and have a great many questions regarding the concept and its practical application. Although they remain skeptical about the idea, they are willing to consider it.

For example, in considering charter schools and the concept of public school choice, Ann Bastian, educator and public choice proponent and senior program officer at the New World Foundation, asks educators to consider eight principles when contemplating charter schools as a form of public school choice. Educators like Bastian counsel that we should reserve the right to suspend judgment on the issue of charter schools and that we should instead focus on the important questions that will help us evaluate public choice as an educational reform. The eight principles she asks us to consider are:

1. Whether a particular charter school strengthens or weakens public education as a whole
2. Whether charters are models that can be replicated or whether they are so unique that other schools have little to learn from them
3. Whether charter schools are truly public and thus nonsectarian
4. Whether charters are really innovative and whether the charter meets an educational need that's not already being met by an existing public school
5. Whether the charter is accountable to the public
6. Whether charters are governed by local schools boards and not some outside authorities such as the state legislature or state department of education
7. Whether in certain key areas, such as funding, teacher licensing, employee rights, and collective bargaining, charters are treated the same as all other public schools, and
8. If charters are being treated as pilots until the public has sufficient evidence to assess the violability of the charter experiment. (Bastian 1996, 45–48)

Bastian, like other educational policymakers, contends that further research and study need to be undertaken before any positions on charter schools can be reasonably formulated. Many educators and politicians conclude that the impact of charter schools on public education as a whole has not been sufficiently studied. These educators point to discrepancies in the studies that do exist and encourage further study and research.

CONCLUSION

The political issues that are involved with the charter school reform movement are controversial, complex, and, because the movement is relatively new, undecided and virtually untested. Although more information is beginning to surface, there still is very little data on the impacts of charter schools on U.S. education, and the data that do exist are not determinative. Because charter schools represent a unique educational reform measure that is local and regional in nature, the challenge in the future will be to examine some of the basic charter claims and assumptions in light of newly emerging evidence. This is difficult because charter laws and charters vary from state to state. Without more data, it is impossible at this point to really gauge the impact of charter schools on public education, but what can be considered are the questions that will need to be asked. Some of these questions might be:

- Will charters disinvest public schools in favor of small, elite enclaves of learning?
- What impact will charters schools have on the desegregation efforts of the last 100 years?
- Will charters exclude students based on subtle admission policies?
- Will charters be able to meet the needs of all students, including special education students?
- What will be the impact on charters in terms of educational accountability? Will charters really raise educational standards and performance?
- Will charters lead to the wholesale loss of public education or will they provide a reform measure as a way to protect public education from privatization?
- Will charter schools really vitalize communities and parental involvement?
- Will charter schools serve to usher in privatization through for-profit management of public schools?
- Will charter schools impact on traditional public schools in ways that allow them to incorporate new and innovative methods in their pedagogical practices?

Those questions, and many more, are just some of the queries that educational stakeholders will need to wrestle with if the impact of charter schools on public education is to be understood. The issues that educational policymakers grappled with at the beginning of the twentieth century—issues such as social functionalism, progressivism, the goals and purposes of education, the education of newly arriving immigrants, multiculturalism, race, culture, and democracy—are still central in the charter movement debate today. In fact, these controversies in one way or another have nurtured the development of charter schools as an educational reform movement. Whether charter schools will live up to their claim to improve all schools in the U.S. public educational system or whether they will remain discrete and elitist enclaves has yet to be decided.

REFERENCES

Bastian, A. "Charter Schools: Potentials and Pitfalls." In *Selling Out Our Schools: Vouchers, Markets, and the Future of Public Education.* Ed. R. Lowe and B. Miner. Milwaukee, WI: ReThinking Schools, 1996.

Bobbitt, F. "The Elimination of Waste in Education." *Elementary School Teacher* 12 (1912): 259–271.

———. "Some General Principles of Management Applied to the Problems of City School Systems." In *Twelfth Yearbook of the National Society for the Study of Education.* Ed. S. C. Parker. Chicago: University of Chicago Press, 1913.

Brown v. Board of Education. 347 U.S. 483, 74 S. Ct. 686. 1954.

Brown v. Board of Education II. 349, U.S. 294, 75, S. Ct. 753. 1955.

Bryk, A., and V. Lee. *Catholic Schools and the Common Good.* Cambridge, MA: Harvard University Press, 1993.

Callahan, R. E. *Education and the Cult of Efficiency.* Chicago: University of Chicago Press, 1962.

Carnegie Foundation for the Advancement of Teaching. *School Choice.* Princeton, NJ, 1992.

"Charter Schools, an Emerging Market." *Florida Trend* (October 1998): 1.

Chubb, J., and T. Moe. *Politics, Markets, and American Schools.* Washington, DC: Brookings Institute, 1990.

Cobb, C., and G. Glass. *Ethnic Segregation in Arizona Charter Schools.* Tempe, AZ: Education Policy Analysis, January 1999.

Corwin, R. G., and J. F. Flaherty, eds. *Freedom and Innovation in California's Charter Schools.* Los Alamitos, CA: Southwest Regional Laboratory, November 1995.

Cubberley, E. *Public School Administration: A Statement of the Fundamental Principle Underlying the Organization and Administration of Public Education.* Boston: Houghton Mifflin, 1916.

Dent, D. "Diversity Rules Threaten North Carolina Charter Schools that Aid Blacks." *New York Times,* 23 December 1998.

Dewey, J. *Education Today.* New York: Greenwood Press, 1940.

———. *Experience and Education.* New York: Collier Books, 1976; first published in 1938.

DuBois, W. E. B. *The Education of Black People: Ten Critiques, 1906–1960.* Ed. H. Aptheker. New York: Monthly Review Press, 1973.

Education Commission of the States. *Action for Excellence: A Comprehensive Plan to Improve Our Nation's Schools.* Washington, DC: Task Force on Education for Economic Growth, 1983.

"For Profit Schools." *Business Week,* 7 February 2000.

Friedman, M. "The Role of Government in Education." In *Economics and the*

Public Interest. Ed. Robert A. Solow. New Brunswick, NJ: Rutgers University Press, 1955.

Goodman, J. "Change without Difference." *Harvard Educational Review* 65, no. 1 (1995): 1–29.

Green v. School Board. 391 U.S. 430 (1968).

Hargreaves, A. *Changing Teachers, Changing Times: Teachers' Work and Culture in the Postmodern Age.* New York: Teachers College Press, 1994.

Huber, R. *The American Idea of Success.* New York: McGraw-Hill, 1971.

Hunt Report. *See* Education Commission of the States.

Hutchins, L. *A+chieving Excellence.* Aurora, CO: Mid Continent Regional Laboratory, 1990.

Kincheloe, J. *Contextualizing Teaching.* New York: Longman, 2000.

Kliebard, H. "The Tyler Rationale." *School Review* 78 (1970): 259–262.

Kolderie, T. *What Does It Mean to Ask: Is "Charter Schools" Working?* St. Paul, MN: Charter Friends National Network, 1998.

Lewin, Tamar. "In Michigan, School Choice Weeds Out Costlier Students." *New York Times,* 26 October 1999.

Lewis, D. L. *W. E. B. DuBois: A Biography of a Race, 1868–1919.* New York: Henry Holt, 1993.

Lopez, A., A. S. Wells, and J. J. Holme. "Bounds for Diversity: Structuring Charter School Communities." Paper presented at the annual meeting of the American Education Research Association, San Diego, April 1998.

Lowe, R., and B. Miner, eds. *Selling Out Our Schools: Vouchers, Markets, and the Future of Public Education.* Milwaukee, WI: ReThinking Schools, 1996.

Lugg, C. A. *For God and Country: Conservatism and American School Policy.* New York: Peter Lang, 1996.

Manetto, N. "Public Schools Touted." *Times* (Trenton, NJ), 4 November 1999.

Meier, D. "The Debate Is about Privatization, Not 'Choice.'" In *Selling Out Our Schools: Vouchers, Markets, and the Future of Public Education.* Ed. R. Lowe and B. Miner. Milwaukee, WI: ReThinking Schools, 1996.

———. *The Power of Their Ideas.* Boston: Beacon Press, 1995.

"Michigan Charter Schools." *ReThinking Schools* (Winter 1999–2000).

Molnar, A. "Charter Schools: The Smiling Face of Disinvestment." *Educational Leadership* 54 (1996): 5.

Nathan, J. *Charter Schools: Creating Hope and Opportunity for American Education.* San Francisco: Jossey-Bass, 1999.

National Science Board. *Educating Americans for the 21st Century.* Washington, DC: Commission on Pre-College Education in Mathematics, Science, and Technology, 1983.

Orfield, G. *The Reconstruction of Southern Education: The Schools and the 1964 Civil Rights Act.* New York: Wiley Interscience, 1969.

Perkinson, L. M. "The History of Blacks in Teaching: Growth and Decline within the Profession." In *American Teachers: Histories of a Profession at Work.* Ed. D. Warren. New York: Macmillan, 1989.

Pratt, C. "Rallying the Troops: Public School Outcry over Charter Plans." *Newsday,* 17 January 2000.

Rinehart, J., and J. Lee. *American Education and the Dynamics of Choice.* New York: Praeger, 1991.

Rofes, E. "Charters: Finding the Courage to Face Our Contradictions." In *Selling Out Our Schools: Vouchers, Markets, and the Future of Public Education.* Ed. R. Lowe and B. Miner. Milwaukee, WI: ReThinking Schools, 1996.

"Saving Our Schools." *Newsweek,* 9 May 1983, 50–58.

Shor, I. *Culture Wars: School and Society in the Conservative Restoration.* Chicago: University of Chicago Press, 1986.

Stent, M., W. Hazard, and H. Rivlin, eds. *Cultural Pluralism in Education: A Mandate for Change.* New York: Appleton-Century Crofts, 1973.

Tyack, D. B. *Constructing Difference: Historical Reflections on Schooling and Social Diversity.* N.p.: Teachers College Record, 1993.

———. *The One Best System: A History of American Urban Education.* Cambridge, MA: Harvard University Press, 1974.

U.S. Department of Education. Joint Committee on Public Schools. Report. December 1999.

U.S. General Accounting Office. *Charter Schools: New Model for Public Schools Provides Opportunities and Challenges.* HEHS-95-42. Washington, DC, January 1995.

U.S. Senate. Committee on Labor and Human Resources. Congressional testimony of Eric Rofes in a hearing on the overview of charter schools. Washington, DC, 31 March 1998.

Urahn, S., and D. Stewart. *Minnesota Charter Schools: A Research Report.* Minneapolis: House Research Department, December 1994.

Vanourek, G., B. Manno, C. Finn, and L. Bierlein. *Charter Schools as Seen by Those Who Know Them Best: Students, Teachers, and Parents.* Charter School in Action Project. Final report, pt. 1. June 1997.

Wells, A., A. Lopez, J. Scott, and J. Holme. "Charter Schools as Postmodern Paradox: Rethinking Social Stratification in an Age of Deregulated School Choice." *Harvard Educational Review* 69, no. 2 (Summer 1999).

Whitty, G., S. Power, and D. Halpin. *Devolution and Choice in Education: The School, the State, and the Market.* Birmingham, Eng.: Open University Press, 1998.

Wirt, F. M., and M. W. Kirst. *Schools in Conflict: The Politics of Education.* 3d ed. Berkeley, CA: McCutchan, 1992.

Young, T., and E. Clinchy. *Choice in Public Education.* New York: Teachers College Press, 1992.

Chapter Six

●← Teachers' Unions and Charter Schools

INTRODUCTION

Whether one believes that teachers' unions are an obstacle to educational reform or that the unions are the driving force for reform, one thing is clear: teachers' unions are one of the most powerful forces in education. How these unions conduct themselves, the issues they embrace, the directions they take, and the challenges they face will help shape the future of education in the United States.

There are over 2.6 million elementary and secondary teachers in the public schools, and more than 85 percent of them are organized into either the National Education Association (NEA) or the American Federation of Teachers (AFT) (Peterson and Charney 1999, 2). In most states, teachers' unions have collective bargaining agreements as their source of power. These agreements are used as a way to ensure that working conditions and salary issues will be bargained for between the union and the local school district, but they are also a way of institutionalizing reforms that improve public education.

Many union opponents argue that institutionalizing reforms is precisely what is not taking place, and they would claim that teachers' unions are really obstacles to reform. Owing to their assumed inflexibility surrounding staffing, evaluation, and teacher working conditions, many opponents of the teachers' unions argue that they are rigid and do not use their collective power to negotiate and foster school improvements. On the contrary, these opponents argue, the unions use their power to protect their self-interests and block significant school reform.

But the criticism of teachers' unions goes far beyond simply arguing that the unions block significant reform. Anti–teachers' union advocates argue that union efforts to prevent the privatization of schools, from the cafeterias to the administration, clearly show that the unions do not have the best interests of the students at heart. Many anti-union reform advocates argue that unions such as the NEA and the AFT actually impede progress because they do not allow private management of schools.

What many anti-union activists have in common is their support for the privatization of schools—a position that the teachers' unions are clearly and adamantly against. In his book *Teacher Unions: How the NEA and AFT Sabotage Reform and Hold Parents, Students, Teachers, and Taxpayers Hostage to Bureaucracy,* Myron Lieberman argues the anti-union reform position quite eloquently. Opposing everything from collective bargaining agreements to contracts that spell out the do's and don'ts of operating a school from day to day, Lieberman states that "the inevitable tendency is to consult the contract before taking action, a mindset that leads inevitably to union control" (Lieberman 1998, 14).

Besides opposition to teachers' unions over the issue of the privatization of schools, another argument put forth by anti-union advocates is that teachers are being held hostage to unions and are not getting their money's worth. By not supporting merit pay, for example, union opponents argue that the best teachers and best instructional strategies are being lost.

The concept of merit pay rests on the assumption of pay for performance, an assumption which argues that teacher pay structures are not sufficiently guided by market mechanisms. The argument is that teachers who are more productive, that is, who do a better job of teaching as reflected by higher test scores, should receive higher pay. The belief rests on the premise that extrinsic rewards, such as higher pay, will enhance school reform and increase the effectiveness of teachers in general.

The AFT and the NEA insist, as do many teachers and community members, that merit pay inappropriately introduces business productivity structures into the field of education. They complain about the divisiveness that merit pay plans promote and argue that such plans pit teacher against teacher, destroying movements toward collaboration that teachers so desperately need to engage in. Also, the unions contend that with merit pay, teachers in low-income districts will be pitted against teachers in more-affluent districts. Other opponents to merit pay argue that the performance results are based on inauthentic state standardized tests, not authentic assessment, and are thus inadequate (Peterson 2000).

Nowhere is the controversy between opponents and supporters of teachers' unions more evident than in the debate over public school choice and charter schools. In a postmodern society that has moved away from industrialism, many charter advocates argue that teachers' unions, as they currently operate, are barriers to innovation and change. Former public school teacher and chair of the California Senate Education Committee, Democrat Gary Hart, reports that "the California Teacher's Association (CTA) brought its immense power against efforts to create a charter law that give teachers freedom to create the kind of school they thought made sense. The CTA would only support a law that retained union authority over charter schools" (Nathan 1996, 97). In his book *Charter Schools,* Joe Nathan makes the statement that

> in most states, teachers unions have tried to prevent the charter school concept from getting a real test. The idea threatens their power and their concept of how public education ought to operate. However, because some legislators of both parties have stood up to this opposition, and because some charter schools are having real, measurable success, some teacher union leaders and members are rethinking their opposition. (Nathan 1996, 93)

Nathan is not alone in criticizing teachers' unions for standing in the way of charter school reform. Lieberman maintains that because these unions will be inextricably involved in the process of designing charter school legislation, they will make sure that the charter schools are not much different than the schools they replace. Arguing that the unions are incapable of promoting change, Lieberman goes on to argue that only entrepreneurial teachers freed from union constraints can accomplish true reform (Lieberman 1998).

Yet the unions would argue that Lieberman has ignored the success of over 700 charter schools already operating with union collaboration. And they would claim that union opponents, like Lieberman, fail to address the differences within unions and how unions themselves are themselves in transition. For example, they contend that the nation's largest teacher union, the NEA, has recently opened five new charter school sites in five separate states (National Education Association 1999).

Many union spokespeople and pro-union charter proponents would argue that their opposition to charter schools is not opposition to the idea but a fear of the loss of collective bargaining and strength among union members as the country embarks on market solutions to social problems. In fact, union supporters would point out that it was the AFT, through its then leader, Albert Shanker, that introduced the notion of charter schools to the public in a 1988 speech given to the National Press Club in Washington, D.C. And although the AFT supports the idea of charter schools, the organization would probably assert that conservatives support charter schools not as an educational reform measure that preserves public schools but because: charters will hasten the advent of vouchers; a charter school policy will undermine the teacher's unions; and charter schools can advance conservative support for deregulation and for allowing the market to reign. Both the NEA and the AFT oppose vouchers and believe that many supporters of educational reforms such as charter schools are disingenuous and really simply wish to abolish the idea of teachers' organizations in favor of market solutions to educational problems.

The opposition to teachers' unions by anti-union charter school advocates is a reflection of the changing historical nature of the educational debate. And while the media attempts to cast the debate over unions as pro-union or anti-union, the debate is far more complex than that and many pro-union proponents of charter schools also argue that unions need to change.

In their book *Taking Charge of Quality,* Charles Kerchner, Julia Koppich, and Joseph Weeres argue that teachers' unions, as they are presently constructed, are antithetical to educational reform. Insisting that we no longer live and work in an industrial society, the authors claim that the agendas of the unions must change. They say that "until recently, teacher unions have focused almost exclusively on conventional job rights and protection issues—ensuring job security and adequate wages, benefits, and working conditions. They have excelled in that arena. As industrial style unions, they have provided teachers with the kinds of benefits they have needed as workers" (Kerchner, Koppich, and Weeres 1998, 11). Although a staunch defender of teachers' unions, Robert Lowe has expressed similar complaints in his study of the Chicago Teacher Federation (CTF) led by Margaret Haley in the early part of the twentieth century:

> Yet despite its [CTF] support for a number of good causes beyond the schools and its opposition to some deleterious reforms within the schools, it [the CTF] prefigured the limitations of contemporary teacher organizations by developing a trade-union mentality that focused too narrowly on protecting jobs, raising wages, and limiting effort. In keeping with that mentality it adopted an oppositional stance to virtually all educational reforms, regardless of merit—a hallmark of teacher unions since. While this resistance has typically been directed against reform initiatives from the top down, in the collective bargaining era it also has meant resistance to efforts to achieve equality of educational opportunity through school desegregation and community control. (Lowe 1999, 85)

As we shall see, the debate over school reform and the role of the teachers' unions are complex and controversial issues, and they defy simplistic characterization.

WHERE UNIONS AND ANTI-UNION CHARTER PROPONENTS AGREE

In the introduction to a report regarding charter schools, the AFT has stated: "The crisis of confidence in public schools is well known. Public agenda polls (1994 and 1995) indicate that most Americans believe that students today are not achieving as well as they could, as well as students from other nations, or as well as they need to for their—and the country's—future success" (American Federation of Teachers 1996a, 1). The report goes on to note:

> Public education is in ferment. There is much dissatisfaction with the current system. Many people believe that the school system is a moribund and highly bureaucratic monopoly—indifferent to criticism, captive to union interests, unwilling to change, and unaccountable to the public. Cries for reform, greater accountability, and more parental choice are everywhere. . . . Thus, in an era of widespread discontent with public education, a belief in the efficacy of competition, and a climate of deregulation and cries for more accountability and local control, it is no accident that we see a growing demand for reforming the education system, in general, and cries for private school vouchers, the privatization of public schools, and the growth of the charter school movement in particular. (American Federation of Teachers 1996, 1)

Those statements are similar to, if not in concert with, statements made by the NEA, the largest teachers' union in the United States. For instance, the NEA has commented:

> Our challenge is clear: Instead of relegating teachers to the role of production workers—with no say in organizing their schools for excellence—we need to enlist teachers as full partners, indeed, as co-managers of their schools. Instead of contracts that reduce flexibility and restrict change, we—and our schools—need contracts that empower and enable. . . . This new collaboration is not about sleeping with the enemy. It is about waking up to our shared stake in reinvigorating the public education enterprise. It is about educating children better, more effectively, and more ambitiously. (Chase 1997)

What both of those statements by the two powerful teachers' unions reflect is the current state of agreement between many anti-union charter school proponents and advocates of teachers' unions. Both anti-union charter school proponents and pro-union charter proponents believe that education is changing rapidly; both parties agree that educational unionism is based on antiquated relations between school administrators and teacher-workers and must be changed; and both agree that schools must change to meet the exigencies of the twenty-first century. Where they disagree is on the form and content of this transition and the role that teachers' unions will play in future relations between teacher-workers, students, parents, and school administrations.

Joe Nathan blames the unions for what he calls "the factory model" of production and management. Nathan argues that teachers' unions promote the idea that seniority should decide who gets a job and, when a layoff occurs, who loses their job (Nathan 1996, 96). According to Nathan, this model results in a situation whereby it is almost impossible to fire a teacher; thus, bad teachers find refuge in a system that protects incompetence. And according to Nathan and others who advance similar arguments, teachers' unions have a vested interest in maintaining their power and therefore oppose charter schools because they threaten that power. Now, they claim, with parents, teachers, politicians, and students embracing the charter concept, teachers' unions realize they cannot defeat the idea and therefore work to weaken the charter laws (Nathan 1996, 96).

Both the AFT and the NEA would disagree. Although they would argue that mechanisms must be put in place to hold teachers accountable, both unions would claim that they are interested in the well-being of students first and foremost and that the protection of teachers is really a means to that well-being. They argue they support charter school legislation but wish to ensure that the legislation promotes the interests of both teachers and students. In fact, the AFT has clearly stated that

> the AFT supports properly structured charter schools as a useful vehicle for school reform. For charter school legislation to be responsible, it must make sure that all children can participate; that the governance structure is collegial, professional, and democratic; that schools operate within the framework of state or nationally established standards, curriculum, and assessments for all students; and, that teachers have the professional authority to find appropriate ways to achieve those standards for their students. (American Federation of Teachers 1996a, 1)

From the unions' standpoint then, they support charter schools if those schools are responsible. And this responsibility clearly includes allowing teachers to have professional authority and governance authority as well as subjecting charter schools to some state or district regulation.

Many anti-union proponents of charter schools argue that teachers' unions continue to play a role in attempting to kill charter school legislation wherever and whenever the need arises and point to numerous instances in which teachers' unions have done so. One such example they cite concerns the state of Minnesota where the charter school proponent, Joe Nathan, has argued that the Minnesota Federation of Teachers (MFT) opposed charter school reform when it first appeared in 1991 (Nathan 1996, 99). Yet a closer examination of the union's position shows that it was more complex and did not reflect opposition to the idea at all.

The MFT passed a resolution stating it would support Minnesota's charter school legislation only if

1. All teachers staffing the school hold a license under the provisions of the Board of Teaching
2. All staff be part of the bargaining unit in the district that authorize [*sic*] the school
3. The school be required to comply with the master agreement of employee groups in the authorizing district and
4. Be it further resolved that only local districts be authorized to establish any style of alternative or chartered schools (Minnesota Federation of Teachers 1991)

Both the AFT and the NEA have been in agreement regarding the above issues. Although they agree with proponents of charter school reform as to the idea charter schools represent, they promote the development of clear and precise criteria to measure what they feel is a responsible charter school and how they feel such schools should operate.

Thus, for the most part, the disagreement between union proponents and many anti-union charter school proponents is not really over the idea of charter schools but over how the idea will be implemented, what laws charter schools will be susceptible to, and how they will operate and be held accountable. These issues are complex and often are not afforded the depth and scrutiny that they deserve. Media treatment of charter schools in this regard often stifles the debate and understanding of the issues by focusing on anti-union or pro-union dichotomies, which actually obfuscates the important issues facing charter schools as an educational reform movement.

Although the NEA supports charter schools as an educational reform initiative, it differs from anti-union charter school advocates on such issues as accountability. For both anti-union charter proponents and pro-union charter proponents, the issue of accountability and the amount and size of state oversight and regulation remain the discerning aspect between the two positions. NEA president Bob Chase has expressed his concern that "charter school laws without adequate accountability measures open the door to gross abuses that hurt students. Charter schools must serve their communities and be fully accountable to taxpayers. Charters can be vehicles for streamlining administration, increasing parental and community involvement, and expanding the menu of education choices and options" (National Education Association 2000, 1).

COMBATING PRIVATIZATION

Perhaps the main interest of teachers' unions with respect to the charter school debate is to maintain and protect the notion of public schools. Both the NEA and the AFT have expressed concern that charter schools could provide the basis for an alternative school system available to a select few—a veritable road to privatization. They argue for a public, common school as a way of sustaining a pluralistic society in which diverse peoples can live together (American Federation of Teachers 1996b). Worrying about the creation of elite enclaves that promise to educate a small portion of U.S. students, teachers' unions have advocated public scrutiny of the idea along with public disclosure and accountability.

The privatization of public schools has been increasing for some time. In fact, "the education industry," a term coined by EdVentures, an investment firm, is now said to total $680 billion in the United States. The stock value of thirty publicly traded educational companies is growing twice as fast as the Dow Jones average, and brokerage firms such as Lehman Brothers and Montgomery Securities have specialists who seek out venture capital for new forms of penetration into what was once exclusively public education (Light 1998, 2). Entrepreneurs see a $700+ billion industry in education and hope to organize schools into chains in order to control staffing and instruction and create financial efficiencies that will curtail and hold down costs.

All of this activity is troubling to teachers' unions, which compare the privatization of education to the privatization of health care. In fact, Wall Street itself has referred to what was once public education as "education maintenance organizations" (EMOs) and seems to be bent on doing for education what health maintenance organizations (HMOs) have done for health care delivery.

And Wall Street is not alone. The education industry and proposals for corporatizing education have the conservative economist Milton Friedman and other heavy hitters on their side. Friedman first proposed vouchers for schools in 1955 and forty years later, in an op-ed piece for the *Washington Post,* Friedman suggested that "such reconstruction [of schools] can be achieved only by privatizing a major segment of the educational system—i.e., by enabling a private-for-profit industry to develop that will . . . offer effective competition to public schools" (Light 1998, 3).

And since the beginning of the 1990s, that is precisely what has occurred. Such EMOs as the Edison Project contract with school districts throughout the country and use taxpayers' funds and some venture capital to run public schools. Many poor school districts that are strapped for funds, and with parents and school boards desperate for help, turn to these private companies to run their schools, design their curricula, and "deliver" instruction.

Bringing profit-oriented interests to bear on what has been a public venture is rigorously opposed by both the AFT and the NEA. The reasons are multiple but essentially boil down to the philosophy that schools should be run for people, not for profit. The commercialism of education, argue the teachers' unions, will further exacerbate an educational divide and will assure that universal education for all children will become dependent on profits and investments. The unions also argue that profit motivation in education would create more inequity between suburban and urban districts and would also create what the Center for Analysis of Commercialism in Education has called "cookie-cutter schools" whose lesson plans are generic, sanitized, and designed for a one-size-fits-all approach to curriculum development. This approach, in turn, would disempower teachers further, reducing them to mere delivery conduits for commercialized education. The unions insist that the one-size-fits-all educational approach would also create new authoritarian rules for teachers and would divorce them further from the conception and development of curriculum and good teaching practices.

Privatization has come to have multiple meanings within the charter school movement as well. Because the teachers' unions are opposed to all forms of privatization, it is important to itemize their disapproval by highlighting the multifaceted aspect of the privatization efforts. Calls for the privatization of education through vouchers are now the centerpiece of the conservative agenda of dismantling public programs and are termed "entitlements." The different forms of privatization and how they correlate with charter schools are of grave interest to the teachers' unions.

Charter School Reliance on Private Resources

In their efforts to start and maintain charter schools, several school founders have been forced to rely on private funds for start-up costs and initial running and operating costs. Paying rent, securing a mortgage, affording the initial cost of insurance, and often the cost of construction, as well as funding the day-to-day operation of a school, are all costly. The organizational structure of the charter school and its relationship to the overall district in which it operates play huge roles in determining the dependency of a charter school on private funds. The more independent a school is from the district, the more it will be forced to pay out of its own budget for everything from insurance to legal fees. And as a recent University of California, Los Angeles (UCLA) study of privatization and education in California found, many start-up schools tend to be small and have a limited student body. An enrollment of 180 students or less may not be enough to pay for capital expenses, salaries, and benefits as well as curricular materials and administrative overhead costs associated with a new school (Wells and Scott 1999). Freedom from district bureaucracy can be costly and can usually mean private fund-raising from community-based, corporate-based, or foundation-based money, and this movement toward privatization is troubling to the teachers' unions.

The UCLA study found that every charter school studied relied in some way on funding from private foundations, the state of California, or the business community. It also found that the wealthier schools were able to rely on parent volunteers to raise money and write grants whereas parents at the lower-income charter schools generally had less time and fewer social networks to help with such activities. As a result, the already overburdened administration and teaching staffs at the low-income charter schools wrote grants and solicited funds in addition to their other responsibilities. Also, these schools' ability to call on parent volunteers meant that teachers in the wealthier schools could concentrate on teaching instead of fund-raising (Wells and Scott 1999, 9).

The UCLA study was also particularly distressing to union advocates because it confirmed that many suburban or wealthy charter schools were able to raise funds from within their own communities. The study also found that in some communities, parents raised staggering sums of money for school programs that did not even exist in the lower-income schools. Using professional and association connections, many wealthier and suburban schools are able to obtain a great deal of monetary support for school programs and resources. Outside collateral collected by local fund-raisers, such events as Tupperware parties, and corporate sponsorships mean that some charter schools have received exorbitant amounts of money while others have not—thus exacerbating the inequities in public education. The study also found that while schools in wealthier communities can rely on local fund-raising, the lower-income schools often rely exclusively on corporate sponsorships, which leaves them beholden to corporations and other outside donors (Wells and Scott 1999, 9).

Another concern expressed by the unions focuses on the private-public partnerships that often provide huge endowments to some schools and not others. Wells Fargo, Apple Computers, and Hewlett Packard represent just a few of the corporations that have engaged in substantial sponsorship through grants. And while many suburban charter schools can count on elaborate donations from such corporations, those in the lower-income districts find they often are left out of the corporate sponsorship loop.

For example, one urban school the UCLA study researched was started by a nonprofit private educational foundation. Foundation employees wrote and presented the charter to the school board, secured a building for the school, recruited students with the help of a community organization, and paid for the remodeling of the school's facilities. The foundation also hired the faculty, selected the members of the school's governing body, and chose the school's curriculum. A question arose as to the role of a "partnership" and "community control" as it appeared that the school was being operated and controlled by the private foundation (Wells and Scott 1999, 11). This situation, argue the teachers' unions, is antithetical to charter claims of fostering community and local decision making among teachers. From the point of view of the teachers' unions, this example of market reform–based policies points to a subtle privatization of education and the disparities that result when schooling is left to the forces of the private market. The unions insist that it is precisely this pernicious and encroaching privatization that is nibbling away at the notion of a common school in the United States.

The Privatization of School Management

According to the NEA, the number of for-profit companies that run public schools is still relatively small—about sixty in the 1997–1998 school year—but such companies are growing by leaps and bounds. And with the growth of charter schools throughout the nation, private, for-profit management companies have found a unique financial opening (National Education Association 1998, 1). The union notes that the companies include Advantage Schools, Inc., of Boston, Massachusetts; Beacon

Education Management of Nashville, Tennessee; Charter School Administration, which runs five schools in Michigan; the Edison Project, of New York; the Tesseract Group, Inc. (formerly Education Alternatives, Inc.), of Minnesota; the Educational Development Corporation, which runs eight schools in Michigan; the Heritage Academy, of Arizona; Horizon Charter, of Arizona; the Leona Group, which runs charter schools in Michigan and Arizona; Mosaica Education, Inc., of Minnesota; and SABIS Education Systems, another Minnesota-based firm (National Education Association 1998).

What charter school laws have done in some, if not most, states is to allow for-profit companies to run publicly funded charter schools. And because of the ambiguity of many charter school laws, which remain silent on the issue of for-profit management of charter schools or actually embrace the idea, it seems that once a school has been granted a charter it can contract out for educational management organization services.

Arizona, Massachusetts, and Michigan have been identified by the NEA as the states that allow the most for-profit management of charter schools (National Education Association 1998, 2). In a study of Arizona charter schools, the report notes:

> Nearly half of Arizona charters are high schools, the majority run by chains such as PPEP TEC High School, Excel Education Centers, Inc., and the Leona Group. These companies take advantage of the fact that Arizona requires high school students to attend only four hours of school a day. They target kids on the margins of traditional public schools—low achievers, discipline problems, truants—with pledges of swift and simple routes to graduation. And many of the companies increase their revenues by running two or three four-hour sessions a day and substituting self-paced computer instruction for a regular teaching staff.

Although the companies claim they can improve student learning as well as make a profit, the evidence seems to indicate the contrary. Little formal research has been done on the efficacy of the for-profit charter schools, but a 1998 report by the NEA states that the companies fall short of their promises (National Education Association 1998).

Education Alternatives, Inc. (EAI), was the pioneer management company and went from managing one school in Miami, Florida; nine schools in Baltimore, Maryland; and the entire Hartford, Connecticut, School District in 1995 to not having a single contract in 1998. Baltimore canceled its EAI contract when student learning in the nine EAI-run schools did not improve even though the company received $20 million more than the city would have normally spent on those schools. The Miami contract was not renewed when students in the EAI school showed no academic improvement compared to students at a publicly run school (Toch 1998, 35–36).

Private for-profit companies are steadily emerging and developing a presence in the charter school movement—indeed, their growth and development is mushrooming. Many of the newest charter schools to be approved in California, for instance, are run and operated by for-profit companies. The Edison Project runs six charter schools in California and as of March 2000 has the capital to expand and is in the process of starting about twenty-five new schools (Wells and Scott 1999, 13). The company's plans include the adoption and management of hundreds, if not thousands, more charter schools.

Contracting Out for Specific Services

The teachers' unions are also wary of contracting out vital school services to private firms. With a host of entrepreneurs literally waiting to take advantage of the educational marketplace, the practice of contracting out specific services such as food services, insurance, curriculum development, maintenance, and networking is growing. And the for-profit companies that wish to enter into the educational marketplace are focusing primarily on charter schools for these contracting opportunities. Unions are especially concerned that public schools are beginning to contract out more and more regular services to these for-profit private firms. Numerous charter schools are avoiding the use of unionized public employees by beginning to contract out such services as district maintenance, and many charters opt to use private landscaping firms because those firms provide workers with no unions and no salary packages, which means the wages and benefits are less costly.

Amy Wells found in her study of one charter school in California that after the school contracted out its maintenance personnel to a private landscape company, the classified staff's union sued the school, arguing that the charter must use district employees. The charter school prevailed in court by successfully defending its right to hire the less-expensive private company to do the gardening and maintenance at the charter school (Wells and Scott 1999, 15). Unions claim that because district maintenance is often provided by minority workers, who, because of their union affiliations, enjoy benefits, adequate compensation, and safe working conditions, the trend to contract out services to for-profit private firms raises disturbing questions about the future of these employees' working conditions and how they will be able to support their families.

In developing strategies for confronting "niche" contracting, i.e., privatization in specific educational arenas, which is now becoming more pervasive, the NEA, for one, is developing strategies and criteria that will judge private sector involvement in contracting out services. Even in light of this opposition and skepticism of private contracting, it is clear that the union has begun to capitulate to some privatization demands and now promotes what it terms "public/private arrangement" (National Education Association 1998).

UNION POSITIONS ON CHARTER SCHOOL LEGISLATION AND DEVELOPMENT

The ways in which privatization interacts with public schools in this time of decentralization are subtle and not generally known to the public, yet the corporatization of public schools is increasing rapidly. There is very little information about what is taking place at the local charter school. Unlike health care, in which case public debate has at least scratched the surface of the issue, public debate and forums for education have not embraced the privatization of public schools as a topic.

Given some of the issues that have been discussed regarding charter schools, the AFT, like the NEA, has established criteria for judging the efficacy of specific charter school legislation in order to protect public education. Their criteria include public accountability for student achievement, accessibility to charter schools by all students, the empowerment of professional educators at the charter schools, local district approval of charter schools, and the conduct of business in accordance with any and all state laws that require that public business of any kind be conducted publicly (American Federation of Teachers 1996b). As charter school legislation can differ state by state, the AFT established strong national criteria for charter schools in order to focus on charter schools in the various states. Understanding the arguments of unions such as the AFT will help shed some light on the teachers' union positions regarding charter schools.

Standards and Accountability

Both the AFT and the NEA agree that charter schools should meet rigorous state standards. They argue in favor of state assessments and call upon all charter schools to be subjected to those assessments from state to state.

The AFT argues that given the current recognition of and emphasis on difference, commonalties within and among public charter schools would disappear if there were no national criteria to assess their accountability. The union worries that with the development of specific charter schools, say African American schools or gender-based schools, the notion of a common curriculum or a common school might disappear. It questions what might happen if students are shifted from one school to another with no consistent curriculum or standards bridging the various schools. Thus, the AFT goes so far as to call for statewide curriculum frameworks and statewide assessment systems, which would be applicable to all schools whether they were charter schools or not (American Federation of Teachers 1996b).

The NEA voices similar concerns, pointing to what it calls three types of accountability that are needed to hold charter schools accountable to the public good. The first accountability concern is fiscal. Fiscal accountability is understood by unions within the day-to-day operations of a particular charter school, and such matters are usually handled by the governing board of the school. Governance and leadership are essential for a successful system of accountability, so the NEA is concerned about governance accountability.

The second criteria is pedagogical. According to the NEA:

> One formal aspect of pedagogical accountability is the use of state mandated exams as overall indicators of school quality. Although formal pedagogical measures are difficult for teachers and administrators to conceptualize and implement, Charter School Initiative Schools are developing assessment and evaluation tools with non-traditional quality indicators aligned with the school's distinct vision and mission. These indicators include character development, service learning, research, autonomous learning, and cultural appreciation. Put another way, the schools are attempting to think about quality education on a broad scale that goes beyond state required standardized testing. (National Education Association 1999, 6)

The third level of accountability is professional accountability, which is concerned with the standards used to assess a teacher's work. The NEA has developed a teacher evaluation system for its sponsored charter schools that allows parents to sit in a classroom and make observations regarding instruction. This activity, according to the NEA, reinforces the notion that teachers are accountable to parents (National Education Association 1999, 7). The NEA also supports an internal accountability system for professional development and accountability.

Advocating peer mentoring, retreats, and volunteerism among teachers and administrators, the NEA claims that it supports a multidimensional professional accountability system for charter schools (National Education Association 1999, 7).

To ensure that the three accountability factors are included as criteria in evaluating charter schools, the NEA launched the Charter School Initiative (CSI) in 1995. This five-year research and development effort was designed to assist the union and its members interested in starting charter schools and to inform the NEA of proactive roles the union can play in school reform efforts. Currently, the CSI movement is working in five school sites: Kailua, Oahu, Hawaii; Norwich, Connecticut; Colorado Springs, Colorado; San Diego, California; and the Maricopa School District in the Phoenix, Arizona, metropolitan area.

In 1996, when assessing state standard development and charter school law requirements, the AFT found that the disparities between state accountability requirements were not only vast but, as the study noted, only eight of the twenty-five states with charter school legislation that were studied had state standards in all four core subjects (English, science, mathematics, and social studies) that met AFT criteria for accountability. Only seven of the twenty-five states required that charter schools meet the state standards for academic accountability. The study also found that although all states were wrestling with the development and refinement of state standards, six states with charter school legislation did not require that charter schools meet state standards (American Federation of Teachers 1996b, 2; also see Appendix A).

From the point of view of the teachers' unions, the issues of accountability and standards are far more complicated than what has been put forth by charter school advocates. The teachers' unions argue that if charter schools are to really demonstrate their success and to have an impact on public school reform, they must show how their students perform on the same assessment tests given to all public school students. Both the AFT and NEA argue that comparison data are essential for determining the progress of any school, let alone charter schools.

As for experimentation and accountability, both unions understand that change takes time. Legislation for charter schools generally gives them three to five years to demonstrate their efficacy, and only a handful of the schools across the United States have been operating for that period of time. Therefore, argue the unions, it is too early to tell if student achievement in these schools is greater than if the children had remained in their traditional public schools. Thus far, state laws do not require the collection of baseline data about charter schools that would be helpful in determining whether the charter schools have lived up to their claims. And, although charter schools offer a wide range of programs, most do not represent choices that are being tried for the first time. Virtually all the educational approaches and strategies that are being tried in charter schools have been around for decades and have been tried in the traditional public schools (American Federation of Teachers 1996c). So, at this juncture, there really are no sufficient data to determine if charter schools are reaching their goals and having a positive effect on public education.

In 1996, the AFT assessed the twenty-five states that had passed charter legislation and found that seventeen of the twenty-five required that charter schools use the same tests as the other schools to determine that students are meeting state goals for learning. From the union's vantage point, the absence of comparison data in eight of those charter schools is highly problematic and indicative of what happens when no standard accountability is required (American Federation of Teachers 1996c, 4; also see Appendix B).

Accessibility to Charter Schools

Both the NEA and the AFT believe that a public education is a human right and should be available to all people regardless of ethnicity, culture, race, gender, or sexual orientation. They argue that the backbone of democracy is built on public schools, and they argue that assessing public school access remains a large issue to be considered when assessing the efficacy of charter schools. Worried about the propensity of charter schools to create a multitiered choice system, which discriminates against some students and not others, both the NEA and the AFT have argued the charter schools must be open to all students—including students with special needs. Furthermore, the unions contend, the charter schools must be tuition free. The AFT agrees that charter schools can be diverse, appeal to different interests and talents that students might have, and offer varied and different educational strategies and instructional methods, but it is also strongly committed to the idea that despite this diversity, each charter school should be publicly open to all students and thus offer true public choice to U.S. students.

These concerns seem to have merit. In testifying at a legislative hearing in Massachusetts, Robin Foley, cochair of the Worchester Advisory Council in that state, noted that while it took approximately twenty minutes for most families to get registered at the county's Seven Hills Charter School, special education families were left to sit for more than two hours. Three months later, she testified that at least two special needs children were not receiving services prescribed by their individualized education plan (McFarlane 1997). The Seven Hills Charter School is one of twenty-five authorized under the state charter law.

Because each state determines whether charter schools will serve targeted populations, impose academic requirements, or be restricted to grade level or program preferences, potential problems can arise as to how these restrictions operate to exclude students. One particularly troubling aspect unions point to is the issue regarding restrictions on attendance at charter schools. This issue often arises with the requirement at some charter schools that parents sign a contract guaranteeing a certain level of parental participation at the school. A common feature of charter schools, the AFT maintains that this clause in many charter school admission requirements can have the deleterious effect of decreasing the enrollment of children from disadvantaged backgrounds. Many working-class families either cannot afford the time off work or do not have the transportation necessary to regularly participate in their children's schools, and the AFT is worried that parental involvement could be used to screen students based on race or socioeconomic class.

Admissions requirements and processes are another way in which charter schools are better able to shape who attends and who does not. Many charter schools operate on a first-come, first-served basis. Some require meetings and an interview with school officials, and the interview can be used to ensure that there is a fit between the charter school and the family. Although this type of screening might not be overt, in explaining the school's culture and through subtle manipulation administrators can steer students toward or away from a particular charter school.

Charter schools argue that admission requirements such as an interview process are essential to their success, arguing that they must filter applicants to ensure they share the same values and beliefs as the school. The schools want an environment in which everybody is committed to the school's goals and vision, and they see admission requirements and intake interviews as ways to construct that environment. In a 1997 study of charter schools in California, it was found that 44 percent of the ninety-eight charter schools surveyed cited student and/or parent involvement and commitment to the school's philosophy as a factor in denying admission. For start-up charter schools, the number was 50 percent; for conversions, it was 39 percent (SRI International 1997).

Another issue that concerns teachers' unions is how tuition or fees can be used to limit accessibility to charter schools. Although charter schools are prohibited from charging tuition, there is no prohibition on donations, and according to an AFT study on charter school legislation, some charter schools are attempting to collect quarterly "donations" from parents (SRI International 1997, 5). Although the donations are supposed to be voluntary, the teachers' unions worry that many parents who cannot or do not wish to contribute may feel intimidated or feel that their children may not be as welcome as other children at the charter school. Both the AFT and the NEA worry that a policy of donations is a thinly veiled attempt to impose tuition in an effort to deny accessibility to some charter schools (see Appendix C).

Teacher Professionalism

High-quality teaching, teacher accountability, and professional development are all essential aspects of quality charter schools. Both NEA policies and AFT policies call for teacher professionalism through the development of high-quality teacher preparation. And while many charter proponents advocate legislation that specifically allows teachers who do not necessarily have a state license, the teachers' unions are adamant proponents of licensing requirements.

Yet teacher professionalism is not relegated merely to licensing and educational development. Involvement in decision making in such issues as curriculum development, the development of instructional strategies and methods, grouping of students, and implementation of instructional strategies all concern the teachers' unions. The unions argue that initial discussions regarding charter schools focused to some degree on the perception of teachers and the educational profession in general as professionals, and charter schools were a mechanism whereby teachers, parents, and students could negotiate with local school boards for the implementation of new and innovative experiments in education (Budde 1989). The NEA, in a 1998 study, found that teachers in charter schools like the freedom that these independent, experimental schools provide (Green 1998).

Yet, the AFT argues that amid all the rhetoric regarding the greater role that teachers play in charter schools and school governance and development, the facts bear little resemblance to the claims. Indeed, the AFT claims that the central role of highly qualified teachers in creating and governing charter schools has actually been undermined and points to two areas of concern—collective bargaining among and by teachers and teacher certification (see Appendix D).

Collective Bargaining and Charter Schools

The AFT found in one study of charter schools that of the twenty-five states that had charter school legislation at the time, fifteen states had passed legislation that prevented, restricted, or was silent regarding the rights of charter school employees to belong to the local school district collective bargaining unit or to be covered by a collective bargaining agreement (American Federation of Teachers 1996b, 8).

For teachers' unions, collective bargaining assures that employees receive retirement and health care benefits, can bargain for salaries, and can participate in the development of school policies and curriculum. Unions across the country have adopted different strategies as to how to bargain collectively with school districts, and the unions argue that eliminating the rights of employees to bargain collectively will not enhance teacher professionalism or student learning. In fact, they say the contrary is true. In schools where teachers have lost the opportunity for collective bargaining, they work more hours and have fewer benefits and lower salaries. Some reform efforts in the area of collective bargaining have occurred as a result of charter school legislation, including allowances for waivers of contract provisions and the application of special contract clauses designed to meet the needs of special programs at charter schools (American Federation of Teachers 2000, 2).

Of course, anti-union charter proponents argue that collective bargaining stymies reform efforts such as charter schools, and charter schools have sought, in many states, to get waivers from contract terms, such as collective bargaining, that did not meet the needs of the staff in those schools. The argument is that unionization is a hindrance to a high-performing school district. The unions, of course, disagree and point to Japan, Germany, and France where there is a greater degree of unionization among educational workers and yet students in those countries outperform the students in schools in the United States where teachers and other educational staff are not nearly as unionized. The unions also make the argument that even within the boundaries of the United States, the performance of students relative to levels of unionization is positive (Eberts and Stone 1984).

Although anti-union charter proponents argue that collective bargaining is a barrier to educational reform, the teachers' unions remain adamant in their contention that attempts to eliminate collective bargaining have less to do with educational reform than with an all-out assault on the teachers' unions themselves.

Teacher Certification

The previously cited AFT report on charter schools found that of the twenty-five states studied, only six required that all teachers be certified to teach in charter schools. Fifteen of the states allowed charter schools to hire noncertified teachers, and most of those fifteen states allowed all teachers in charter schools to be noncertified. However, Louisiana caps noncertified teachers at 25 percent of the teacher workforce; Delaware allows 35 percent of the teacher workforce to be noncertified; and Connecticut and New Hampshire permit up to 50 percent of the teachers to be noncertified (American Federation of Teachers 1996b, 9).

Proponents of hiring noncertified teachers to teach in charter schools argue that opening the profession to many people talented in their own field would allow for improvement and innovation of teaching and learning. They point to the many retired professionals who wish to work with young minds in educational settings and argue that rigid teacher certification requirements prevent such people from teaching, which, in turn, they argue, hurts the students.

Yet the teachers' unions argue that it is not enough for an educator to know his or her subject matter. It is crucial, they insist, that educators have knowledge about how students learn and how to teach. Simply being knowledgeable in one's field, the teachers' unions argue, does not guarantee that students will gain knowledge. They claim that in order to be an effective educator, teachers must have background knowledge of child development, learning strategies, cognitive theories, and learning assessment. For this reason, they are adamant in their struggle to ensure that every state require that teachers be certified. And although the unions would agree that the certification requirements themselves need to be scrutinized and are less than perfect, at a minimum the requirements guarantee that teachers have been exposed to some courses and experiences that will help them teach students. The unions contend that reforming and strengthening certification requirements, not abandoning the requirements, is preferred (American Federation of Teachers 1996b, 9).

Local District Approval of Charter Schools

One of the arguments put forth in support of charter schools is they will help local school districts by providing competition, which, in turn, will force the traditional public schools to change the way they educate students. The teachers' unions, on the other hand, argue that if a charter school is isolated from the local district in which it operates the effect is fragmentation, which makes the achievement of common standards, supported by the unions, difficult if not impossible. Making charter schools the subject of local district approval, argue the AFT and the NEA, is crucial to making sure that local districts do not ignore the charter schools. Because some advocates of charter schools argue that local districts are reluctant to grant charters to applicant schools, the AFT maintains that to ensure a fair hearing to applicants and to promote a strong collaboration with and connection to local districts, charter school legislation should include an appeal process (American Federation of Teachers 1996b, 11).

Avoiding obstructionism by local school districts while at the same time requiring the local education agency to grant charters is the goal of the AFT and the NEA. These unions argue that the charter legislation should contain language that identifies and specifically indicates requirements for public notice and public hearings as well as guidelines for approval or denial. The unions feel that public oversight and monitoring are essential to the success of charter schools. According to the NEA:

> The theory that underlies charters is that such freeing of public schools will hasten educational innovation, improve student achievement, create greater parental involvement, and promote improvement of public education in general. And the theory provides that if there's no educational improvement, the school will be held accountable and the school's charter won't be renewed. Thus, careful public oversight and accurate accountability measures are critical to the whole hypothesis of charter schools. (National Education Association 2000, 2)

However, of the twenty-five states studied by the AFT in 1996 that had passed charter legislation, only Arizona and Massachusetts bypassed the local education agency completely in granting charters. Seven states permitted other entities such as universities and state departments to grant charters in addition to local agencies. Colorado and North Carolina had a process spelled out in their charter legislation that allowed the charter applicant to appeal to the state should a charter not be granted by the local education agency (American Federation of Teachers 1996b, 11).

Public Accountability and Charter Schools

Both the NEA and the AFT are avid supporters of what are termed "sunshine laws." Most states have these laws, which are designed to ensure that all public business is conducted in the open. The AFT and NEA contend that because charter schools are public schools, all meetings regarding the business of these schools should be open to public scrutiny. They claim that all information about a charter school, from its finances to its academic results, should be available to the general public. Yet as the AFT has noted:

Accountability requirements differ widely from state to state. Although many states require charters to submit to an annual report, the states fail to define the contents of the report or require that the reports be made available to the public. Most states require annual audits to be submitted but fail to define the contents of those reports. Other states require charters to submit the same reports that district schools are required to submit. . . . Our analysis of current charter school legislation, like our 1966 study, reveals considerable variation from state to state. (American Federation of Teachers June 1999, 2)

From the point of view of the AFT and the NEA, variation from state to state provides no ability to set standards, no benchmarking ability, and thus no way to hold schools accountable. Setting guidelines for accountability procedures, argue the unions, is essential to monitor charter schools and allow public oversight. At a minimum, maintains the AFT, states and/or the local communities in which charter schools are operating should be required to issue an annual report that includes information concerning:

- How many charters there are and where they are located
- Who attends the charter schools—demographic information about the student body, and information as to whether special needs students are enrolled
- Who staffs these schools—the credentials of staff members
- The student and staff turnover rate
- The composition of the education program
- Student performance on achievement tests used by the state and/or designed to assess progress of students in meeting state standards
- Where the money comes from—a full accounting of all sources of revenues and
- How the money has been spent—a financial accounting of all expenditures. (American Federation of Teachers 1996b, 12)

TRANSFORMING TEACHERS' UNIONS: RETHINKING ROLES AND RESPONSIBILITIES

In order to head in a new direction and to embrace the emerging needs of our nation's children, many progressives argue that the teachers' unions must also change. They argue that unions must create and maintain a vision of equity for all students; that they must seek to defend public education and the rights of teachers; that teachers' unions must place a strong emphasis on professionalism and accountability; and that these unions must be committed to all children in the communities they serve by addressing issues of race, class, and gender discrimination if they mean that some students are excluded and others rewarded (Peterson and Charney 1999).

With the rapid changes in the knowledge needs of citizens, education is changing in both form and content. Teachers' unions are one of the most powerful forces in education, and the direction they take will determine to some degree the nature of education and educational opportunities in the United States. Progressive educators argue that teachers' unions must begin to be involved with issues of social justice and anticorporate posturing. Many progressive educators believe that privatization efforts constitute an all-out attack on public education and that this form of corporatization is taking place, not just in the arena of education, but in society at large. They argue that if teachers' unions are to transcend the past and truly embark on a road of social justice and equity for all students, they must join with other anticorporate and antiprivatization efforts that are taking place throughout the country.

Along with allying with others to achieve social justice, progressive educators argue that teachers' unions must, at a minimum, be implicated in:

- Determining who enters the teaching profession
- Designing mentoring programs where new teachers receive intensive guidance and help
- Participating in community outreach programs where teachers use public forums such as churches, temples, community centers, sororities, and such for purposes of engaging community members in supporting educational efforts
- Developing self-monitoring measures that would assure that all teachers perform with high quality
- Operating a teachers' development center where teachers teach and receive educational units for their efforts
- Designing programs that combat prejudice and racism and incorporating multicultural and gender concerns into the curriculum
- Working in an ongoing alliance with community members, unions from other professions, youth groups, and public organizations in efforts to transform social maladies
- Holding membership meetings in an atmosphere of civility and

inquiry whereby social issues could be addressed in more systematic and comprehensive ways. (Peterson and Charney 1999, 14)

This professional unionism, progressive educators contend, must maintain a focus on innovative reforms such as charter schools while remaining vigilant in its opposition to privatization. And, claim progressive educators, this professional unionism must be a social justice unionism grounded in a commitment to global and national struggles that go beyond the classroom into the community at large.

Nowhere is the issue of professional unionism more obvious than in the area of teacher accountability. Although accountability has been the focus of many anti-union advocates, social justice unionism would focus on transcending the industrial model whereby accountability is the responsibility of principles and supervisors, not teachers. Professional accountability, argue progressive educators, must look beyond simply individual teachers and their individual rights and also consider the broader issues facing teachers. Internal quality controls, argue professional union advocates, would transcend the industrial model of teachers' union relations while at the same time assuring that due process and collective bargaining stay intact.

The people who seek to transform unions, as opposed to abolishing or destroying them, argue that the unions need to:

- Define and measure quality—for students, teachers, and schools
- Organize around individual schools and abandon school district organizing
- Focus on building an external labor market for teachers that would allow them to keep their benefit protections and employment support services as they move from job to job, in or out of the district
- Enable teachers to take roles traditionally left to district administrators
- Support teachers in developing their skills
- Award teachers higher salaries by creating incentives for acquiring new skills and expertise
- Develop new strategies for ensuring employment security
- Actively involve teachers in planning, policymaking, and resource allocation
- Redefine teaching
- Create standards for student performance
- Institute peer assistance
- Redefine curriculum and transform schools. (Kerchner, Koppich, and Weeres 1998, 12–13)

SUMMARY

Teachers' unions have been one of the most successful union efforts in the twentieth century. They have fought for professionalism and collective bargaining arrangements that have transformed education. How charter schools are run, the legislation they operate under, and the accountability demanded of them will all be decided, in part, with the help of the teachers' unions. If the unions can advocate successfully for students and accept new forms of innovation and experimentation, they will succeed in transforming themselves and the teachers in them. Charter schools provide one of the challenges and opportunities that the teachers' unions will face as we enter the twenty-first century.

REFERENCES

American Federation of Teachers. *AFT Charter Report.* Washington, DC, 1996a.
——. *AFT's Criteria for Good Charter School Legislation.* Washington, DC, 1996b.
——. *Charter School Update.* Educational Policy Issues Policy Brief, no. 9. Washington, DC, June 1999.
——. *State by State Analysis of Charter School Legislation.* Washington, DC, 25 February 2000.
——. *What We Know about Charter Schools.* Washington, DC, 1996c.
Budde, R. *Education by Charter: Restructuring Schools and School Districts.* Andover, MA: Regional Laboratory for Educational Improvement of the Northeast and Islands, 1989.
Chase, Bob. "The New Unionism: A Course for School Quality." Speech given by the president of the National Education Association to the National Press Club, 5 February 1997.
Cotton, Lynyonne. *Charter School Initiative.* Washington, DC: Howard University, August 1999.
Eberts, R., and A. Stone. *Unions and Public Schools.* Lexington, MA: Lexington Books, 1984.
Green, R. "Union Research Finds Teachers Pleased with Charters." Associated Press, 2 July 1998.
Kerchner, C., J. Koppich, and J. Weeres. *Taking Charge of Quality: How Teachers and Unions Can Revitalize Schools.* San Francisco, CA: Jossey-Bass, 1998.
Lieberman, M. *Teacher Unions: How the NEA and the AFT Sabotage Reform and Hold Parents, Students, Teachers, and Taxpayers Hostage to Bureaucracy.* Washington, DC: Education Policy Institute, 1998.

Light, Julie. "The Education Industry: The Corporate Takeover of Public Schools." *Corporate Watch,* 8 July 1998.

Lowe, R. "The Chicago Teacher's Federation and Its Legacy." In *Transforming Teacher Unions: Fighting for Better Schools,* 14. Ed. B. Peterson and M. Charney. Milwaukee, WI: ReThinking Schools, 1999.

McFarlane, C. "Charter Schools Facing Scrutiny over Special Education." *Telegram and Gazette* (Worcester, MA), 1 April 1997.

Minnesota Federation of Teachers. "Minutes of Executive Council Meeting, 20 April 1991."

Nathan, J. *Charter Schools: Creating Hope and Opportunity for American Education.* San Francisco, CA: Jossey-Bass, 1996.

National Education Association. *Charter Schools: NEA Calls for Stronger School Laws to Spur Innovation.* Washington, DC, 3 April 2000.

———. *Charter Schools Run by For-Profit Companies.* Washington, DC, 23 April 2000.

———. *Education, Investors, and Entrepreneurs: A Framework for Understanding Contracting-Out Public Schools and Public School Services.* Washington, DC, 1998.

———. *In Brief: For-Profit Management of Public Schools.* Washington, DC, 1998.

Peterson, B. "Merit: To Pay or Not to Pay." *ReThinking Schools* 14, no. 3 (Spring 2000): 1.

Peterson, B., and M. Charney, eds. *Transforming Teacher Unions: Fighting for Better Schools and Social Justice.* Milwaukee, WI: ReThinking Schools, 1999.

SRI International. *Evaluation of Charter School Effectiveness.* Report prepared for the state of California Office of Legislative Analyst. Menlo Park, CA, 1997.

Toch, T. "Education Bazaar." *U.S. News and World Report,* 27 April 1998, 35–36.

Wells, A., and J. Scott. "Evaluation of Privatization and Charter Schools." UCLA charter school study prepared for Conference on the National Center for the Study of Privatization in Education, New York, Columbia University Teachers College, April 1999.

Chapter Seven

⚭ Organizations, Associations, and Government Agencies

The following are organizations, associations, and governmental agencies that provide information on charter schools and the charter school controversies.

American Federation of Teachers
555 New Jersey Avenue, NW
Washington, DC 20001
202-393-8642
www.aft.org

One of the largest teachers' unions in the United States, the American Federation of Teachers (AFT) is a good source for information about union positions regarding charter schools and activities in specific areas of the United States.

American Institutes for Research
3333 K Street, NW
Washington, DC 20007-3541
202-342-5000
www.air-dc.org

The American Institutes for Research (AIR) is an independent, nonprofit organization that provides government and the private sector with services that promote high quality by applying and advancing the knowledge, theories, methods, and standards of the behavioral and social sciences to solve significant societal problems. Institutes are located throughout the United States, and AIR is responsible for research on charter schools.

Annenberg Institute for School Reform
Brown University
Box 1985
Providence, RI 02912
401-863-7990
http://home.aisr.Brown.edu

The mission of the Annenberg Institute for School Reform is to develop, share, and act on knowledge that improves the conditions and outcomes of schooling in the United States, especially in urban communities and in schools serving underserved children. The institute currently focuses its programs in six initiative areas. It carries out its work through research and analysis, collaborations with partner organizations, support for local action, publications, and conferences. To help develop and refine its programming, the institute periodically convenes a program advisory group to review current activities and make recommendations for the future focus of the institute's work.

Association of Educators in Private Practice
N7425 Switzke Road
Watertown, WI 53094
800-252-3280
e-mail: info@aepp.org

The Association of Educators in Private Practice (AEPP) is a growing nonprofit, national, and professional organization made up of private practice educators. The group's mission is based on providing support for and advancement of the education of students; aiding and assisting educators in private practice in the performance of their lawful functions; enhancing the effectiveness and professionalism of educators in private practice; encouraging, sponsoring, and facilitating the intercommunication and sharing of ideas and issues identified as common and relevant to educators in private practice; and promoting the instruction and training of an educated citizenry. AEPP publishes a variety of materials for members and nonmembers, including an *Index of Opportunities,* an *AEPP Directory,* and a newsletter entitled *Enterprising Educators,* which is published in the fall and spring.

Center for Critical Thinking
Sonoma State University
P.O. Box 220
Dillon Beach, CA 94929
707-878-9100; fax: 707-878-9111
www.criticalthinking.org

The Center for Critical Thinking conducts advanced research and disseminates information on critical thinking. Each year it sponsors an international conference on critical thinking and educational reform. It has worked with the college board, the National Education Association, the U.S. Department of Education, and numerous colleges, universities, and school districts to facilitate the implementation of critical thinking instruction focused on intellectual standards.

Center for Education Reform
1001 Connecticut Avenue, NW, Suite 204
Washington, DC 20036
202-822-9000
www.edreform.com

The Center for Education Reform is a conservative organization that publishes newsletters and materials about education reform, including charter schools. It has links on its website to various federal and state educational agencies, and it provides research and guidance for those interested in education reform.

Center for Research on Evaluation, Standards, and Student Testing (CRESST)
CRESST/University of California, Los Angeles
Box 951522
300 Charles E. Young Drive
North Los Angeles, CA 90095-1522
310-206-1532; fax: 310-825-3883
www.ed.org

Funded by the U.S. Department of Education and the Office of Educational Research and Improvement, the Center for Research on Evaluation, Standards, and Student Testing (CRESST) conducts research on important topics related to educational testing from kindergarten through grade twelve.

Center for School Change
Humphrey Institute, University of Minnesota
301 Nineteenth Avenue South
Minneapolis, MN 55455
612-626-1834
e-mail: jnathan@hhh.umn.edu

The Center for School Change publishes reports on the concept of charter schools, policies that underlie the movement, and the laws that govern it. It is a useful source for anyone who is trying to create a charter school.

Center on Reinventing Public Education
University of Washington, Box 363060

Seattle, WA 98195-3060
206-685-2214
e-mail: correspondence@rand.org

The Center on Reinventing Public Education seeks to develop and evaluate methods of public oversight that can allow individual schools to be focused, effective, and accountable. The center's research program, which was established in 1993, centers on current governance arrangements in public education, and researchers have found that the most productive schools follow coherent instructional strategies in an environment free of regulation and compliance imperatives. The center pursues a national program of research and development on such proposals as charter schools, school contracting, school choice, and school system decentralization via alliances with the Brookings Institute, the RAND Corporation, Vanderbilt University, and the University of Chicago. The center also conducts research into reform initiatives in Washington State and the Seattle public schools.

Charter Schools Development Center
California State University Institute for Education Reform
California State University, Sacramento
6000 J Street
Sacramento, CA 95819-6018
916-278-4611
www.csus.edu
e-mail: epremach@calstate.edu

The Charter Schools Development Center (CSDC) is a nonprofit program housed at California State University at Sacramento. CSDC's goal is to help public education make the leap from being a highly regulated, process-based system to one that allows and encourages schools to be more creative, performance-based centers of effective teaching and learning. The center provides technical assistance to the charter school reform movement in California and nationally. Its staff has extensive hands-on experience in both charter school policy and school-based practice, and staff members are known for their in-depth and practical expertise in the most challenging aspects of charter school planning, operations, and oversight. They specifically provide assistance in how to plan and start a charter school; how to define and measure student and school performance; how to understand the roles and responsibilities of charter-granting agencies; and how to understand charter school finance and operations, school governance and leadership, and charter school laws and policy.

Coalition of Essential Schools
1814 Franklin Street, Suite 700
Oakland, CA 94612
510-433-1451
www.essentialschools.org

The Coalition of Essential Schools is a growing national network of over 1,000 schools and twenty-four regional support centers. It has evolved from a centrally run organization to a decentralized network of regional centers that provide technical assistance and personalized support to schools.

Consortium for Policy Research in Education
Graduate School of Education, Pennsylvania State University
University Park, PA 16802
814-863-2599
www.gv.psu.edu

The Consortium for Policy Research in Education (CPRE) was created in 1985 to bring together researchers from five of the leading universities to improve elementary and secondary education through research on policy, finance, school reform, and school governance. CPRE focuses on three essential components of educational reform: incorporating a coherent set of policies and practices in education, maintaining meaningful incentives for individuals and the organization, and building the capacity of the individual and the organization to institute and sustain necessary changes.

Consortium on Inclusive Schooling Practices
1 Allegheny Center, Suite 510
Pittsburgh, PA 15212-4772
412-359-1600; fax: 412-359-1601
www.asri.edu.org

The Consortium on Inclusive Schooling Practices represents a collaborative effort to enlarge the capacity of state and local education agencies to serve children and youth, with and without disabilities, in school and community settings. The focus of the project is on systemic reform rather than on changes in special education systems only.

The consortium supports three broad goals: to establish a change process in multiple states focused on systemic reform; to translate research and policy information into educational practices that can be implemented; and to develop the capacity of state and local agencies to provide inclusive educational services.

Council of Chief State School Officers
1 Massachusetts Avenue,
NW, Suite 700
Washington, DC 20001-1431
202-408-5505
www.ccsso.org

The Council of Chief State School Officers (CCSSO) is a nationwide, nonprofit organization composed of public officials who head the departments responsible for elementary and secondary education in the states, nonstate U.S. jurisdictions, the District of Columbia, and the Department of Defense's Education Activity Committee. In representing chief education officers, the CCSSO works on behalf of the state agencies that serve public school students throughout the nation. It hosts council partnerships, helps implement federal education programs, endorses council projects, and issues publications and news releases concerning educational reform efforts.

Council of the Great City Schools
1301 Pennsylvania Avenue,
NW, Suite 702
Washington, DC 20004
www.cgcs.org
202-393-2427

The Council of the Great City Schools is a coalition of some fifty-seven of the nation's largest urban public school systems. Founded in 1956 and incorporated in 1961, the council works to promote urban education through legislation, research, media relations, management, technology, and special projects. The council serves as a voice for urban educators, provides ways to share information about promising practices, and addresses common concerns.

Council of Urban Boards of Education
1680 Duke Street
Alexandria, VA 22314
703-838-6720
e-mail: cube@nsba.org

The Council of Urban Boards of Education was started in 1967 to address the unique needs of school board members serving the largest cities in the United States. The council gathers information, develops recommendations, and takes appropriate action to improve the quality and equality of education.

**Drexel University Foundations Technical
Assistance Center for Public Charter Schools**
133 Q Gaither Drive
Mount Laurel, NJ 08054
888-693-6675; 856-642-6330
www.drexel.edu

Drexel University Foundations Technical Assistance Center for Public Charter Schools (TAC) advocates and assists in the development of quality public charter schools in the mid-Atlantic region as well as the rest of the nation. TAC fosters school improvement by providing technical support to charter school planning groups, application-writing groups, and operating charter schools. Additionally, TAC provides on-site expert educational leaders, makes referrals, conducts workshops and conferences, and promotes legislation for charter schools.

Education Commission of the States
707 Seventeenth Street, #2700
Denver, CO 80202-3427
303-299-3600
www.ecs.org

The Education Commission of the States (ECS) launches partnerships between corporate leaders and education policymakers to help shape the future of public education. The ECS provides initiatives on teacher quality, information about educational reforms, the latest news releases regarding issues in public education, and policy studies. The mission of the ECS is to help state leaders identity, develop, and implement a public policy for education that addresses current and future needs of a learning society.

FairTest
342 Broadway
Cambridge, MA 02139
617-864-4810; fax 617-497-2224
e-mail: info@fairtest.org

FairTest, the National Center for Fair and Open Testing, is an advocacy organization working to end the abuses, misuses, and flaws of standardized testing and to ensure that any evaluation of students and workers is fair, open, and educationally sound.

The center places special emphasis on eliminating the racial, class, gender, and cultural barriers to equal opportunity posed by standardized tests and seeks to prevent any damage they might do to the quality of education. Based on four goals and principles, the center provides information, technical assistance, and advocacy services on a broad range of testing concerns. The focus is on three areas: kindergarten through grade twelve, university admissions, and employment tests, including teacher testing.

Little Hoover Commission
925 L Street, Suite 805
Sacramento, CA 95814
916-445-2125
e-mail: littl.hoover@lhc.ca.org

The Little Hoover Commission is an independent state body that functions to promote efficiency, effectiveness, and economy in California state programs. The commission studies California legislation, publishes reports on state programs, and researches issues such as charter schools.

Morrison Institute for Public Policy
School of Public Affairs, Arizona State University
P.O. Box 874405
Tempe, AZ 85287-4405
480-965-4525
www.asu.edu

The Morrison Institute for Public Policy, located at Arizona State University, researches public policy issues, informs policymakers, and advises leaders on choices and actions in the area of education. The institute provides information and expertise on issues in school reform.

National Center for Fair and Open Testing. *See* **FairTest**

National Center on Education and the Economy
P.O. Box 10391
Rochester, NY 14610
888-361-6233
e-mail: info@ncee.org

The National Center on Education and the Economy concentrates on helping states and localities develop the capacity to design and implement their own education and training systems, systems that are suited to their history, culture, and unique needs. The center does not provide designs to be replicated; it provides resources for design.

National Center on Educational Outcomes
University of Minnesota
350 Elliott Hall
75 East River Road
Minneapolis, MN 55455
612-626-1530; fax: 612-624-0879
www.coledumn.edu

The National Center on Educational Outcomes was established in 1990 to provide national leadership in the identification of outcomes, indicators, and assessments to monitor educational results for all students, including students with disabilities.

National Clearing House for Bilingual Education
George Washington University Center for the
Study of Language and Education
2011 Eye Street, NW, Suite 200
Washington, DC 20006
202-467-0867
www.ncbe.gwu.edu

The National Clearing House for Bilingual Education (NCBE) is funded by the U.S. Department of Education's Office of Bilingual Education and Minority Languages Affairs to collect, analyze, and disseminate information relating to the effective education of linguistically and culturally diverse learners in the United States. NCBE provides information through its website; produces a biweekly news bulletin, *Newsline;* and manages a topical electronic discussion group, NCBE Roundtable. As part of the U.S. Department of Education's technical assistance and information network, NCBE works with other service providers to provide access to high-quality information to assist states and local school districts in the development of programs and the implementation of strategies that will help all students work toward high academic standards.

National Coalition of Advocates for Students
100 Boylston Street, Suite 737
Boston, MA 02116
617-357-8507
e-mail: ncasmfe@mindspring.com

The National Coalition of Advocates for Students (NCAS) is a national nonprofit education and advocacy organization with twenty member groups in fourteen states. NCAS works to achieve equal access to quality public education for students who are most vulnerable to school failure, and its constituencies include low-income students; members of racial, ethnic, and/or language minority groups; recent immigrants; migrant farmworkers; and students with disabilities. Focusing on kindergarten through grade twelve, NCAS informs and mobilizes parents, concerned educators, and communities to help resolve critical education issues. Utilizing national projects and studies, public hearings, and outreach through publications and the media, NCAS raises concerns that otherwise might not be heard.

National Conference of State Legislatures
444 North Capitol Street, NW, Suite 515
Washington, DC 20001
202-624-5400
www.info@ncsl.org

The National Conference of State Legislatures provides legislative updates regarding charter school arguments, research, legislation, and trends.

National Educators Association
1201 Sixteenth Street, NW
Washington, DC 20036
202-833-4000
e-mail: kbrilliant@nea.org

The National Educators Association is a federal organization of educators that is devoted to providing assistance and information regarding the state of public education in the United States.

New American Schools
1560 Wilson Boulevard, Suite 901
Arlington, VA 22209
703-908-9500; fax: 703-908-0622
e-mail: info@nasdc.org

New American Schools is a dynamic coalition of teachers, administrators, parents, policymakers, community and business leaders, and experts from around the country who are committed to improving academic achievement for all students.

The coalition works to change U.S. classrooms, schools, and school systems using designs—blueprints for reorganizing an entire school rather than a single program or grade level within it—and by providing assistance to help schools implement the designs successfully.

New York Charter School Resource Center
41 Robbins Avenue
Amityville, NY 11701
516-598-4426
www.nycharterschools.org

The New York Charter School Resource Center provides services for anyone interested in beginning a charter school in New York State. Its services include explaining and interpreting the state's charter law; helping potential school operators complete and submit charter applications; providing technical assistance for school design, curriculum, standards, and assessment; providing legal services; and maintaining data bases on charter school activity throughout the United States.

Pacific Research Institute for Public Policy
755 Sansome Street, Suite 450
San Francisco, CA 94111
415-989-0833
www.pacificresearch.org

The Pacific Research Institute for Public Policy promotes the principles of individual freedom and personal responsibility. The institute believes these principles are best encouraged through policies that emphasize a free economy, private initiative, and limited government. By focusing on public policy issues such as education, the environment, law, economics, and social welfare, the institute strives to foster a better understanding of the principles of a free society among leaders in government, academe, the media, and the business community.

Progressive Policy Institute
Education Section
600 Pennsylvania Avenue, SE, Suite 400
Washington, DC 20003
202-546-0007
www.dlcppi.org

The mission of the Progressive Policy Institute is to define and promote a new progressive politics for the United States in the twenty-first century. Through its research, policies, and perspectives, the institute is fashioning a new governing philosophy and agenda for public innovation geared to the information age.

Project Zero
Harvard Graduate School of Education

321 Longfellow Hall
13 Appian Way
Cambridge, MA 02138
617-496-7097
pzweb.harvard.edu

Project Zero, a research group in the Harvard Graduate School of Education, has investigated the development of learning processes in children, adults, and organizations for over thirty-two years. Today, Project Zero is building on this research to help create communities of reflective, independent learners; to enhance deep understanding within disciplines; and to promote critical and creative thinking. Project Zero's mission is to understand and enhance learning, thinking, and creativity in the arts and other disciplines for individuals and institutions.

Regional Educational Laboratories
222 Richmond Street, Suite 300
Providence, RI 02903-4226
401-274-9548
www.ncrel.org

The Regional Educational Laboratories have ten networks serving geographic regions that span the nation. They work to ensure that people involved in educational improvement efforts at the local, state, and regional levels have access to the best available information from research and practice. With support from the U.S. Department of Education, the Regional Educational Laboratories work with state and local educators, community leaders, and policymakers to tackle difficult problems in education.

ReThinking Schools: An Urban Educational Journal
1001 E. Keefe Avenue
Milwaukee, WI 53212
414-964-9646
www.rethinkingschools.org

ReThinking Schools: An Urban Education Journal is a nonprofit, independent journal advocating the reform of elementary and secondary public schools. Emphasis is placed on urban schools and issues of social justice, and the journal stresses a grassroots perspective combining theory and practice and linking classroom issues to broader policy concerns. It is an activist publication and encourages teachers, parents, and students to become involved in building quality public schools for all children. The journal is published by Milwaukee-area teachers and educators, and contributing writers are from around the country. *Re-Thinking Schools* focuses on local and national school reform.

SERVE Leaders Institute
P.O. Box 5406
Greensboro, NC 27435
336-334-4729
www.serve.org

The SERVE Leaders Institute is funded by a U.S. Department of Education grant, and its purpose is to address the challenges that charter school innovators and leaders face in the charter school reform movement. The institute arranges retreat activities with the assistance of nationally recognized charter school leaders. The leadership program is based on and expands the understanding of educational training programs, continuous learning, result-driven evaluation models, and practical issues that face educators daily.

Southwest Educational Development Laboratory
211 East Seventh Street
Austin, TX 78701-3281
800-476-6861
www.sedl.org

The Southwest Educational Development Laboratory works to meet the information needs of decision makers and policymakers as they create policies to improve education in their states and localities. The laboratory focuses on basic areas of direct services and applied policy research and development. It offers policy, practical, and research information about priority education topics, advice on how to discuss educational issues, in-depth studies on charter schools, and information about charter school legislation. It also provides resources such as policy briefs, meeting summaries, and articles that address the topic of charter schools and other educational reform issues.

Thomas Fordham Foundation
Manhattan Institute
52 Vanderbilt Avenue, Second Floor
New York, NY 10017
212-599-7000
e-mail: fordham@dunst.com

The Thomas Fordham Foundation supports research, publications, and projects of national significance in elementary and secondary education reform as well as significant education reform projects in Dayton, Ohio, and vicinity. The foundation is affiliated with the Manhattan Institute, a think tank whose mission is to design, develop, and make available information on educational reform.

Chapter Eight

● Selected Print and Nonprint Resources

The works listed in this chapter are divided into two categories. The first lists both popular and scholarly books, articles, speeches, and studies that deal with the topic of educational reform and, specifically, charter schools. These include law journals, labor reports, government publications, and books by individual authors. The second section contains nonprint resources such as websites and internet research sites.

PRINTED SOURCES

Union Publications

The following publications are published by the American Federation of Teachers (AFT) and the National Education Association (NEA). The speeches by Albert Shanker, former AFT president, are also available through the AFT. The AFT can be reached by contacting its website, www.aft.org, or by writing to the American Federation of Teachers, 555 New Jersey Avenue, NW, Washington, DC 20001. The NEA has developed a charter school initiative with Andrea DiLorenzo and Kay Brilliant as its codirectors. They can be reached at adilorenzo@nea.org or kbrilliant@nea.org, or by writing to them directly at Charter School Initiative, Public Education Advocacy Center, National Education Association, 1201 Sixteenth Street, NW, Washington, DC 20036.

American Federation of Teachers. *The AFT Charter School Report.* Washington, DC, 2000.

In this report, the union issues what could be called "a report card" on charter schools. The publication examines the issue state by state.

American Federation of Teachers. *Charter School Briefing Packet.* Washington, DC, 1995.

A comprehensive report on what charter schools are doing and in which specific localities. The report contains controversies and critiques.

American Federation of Teachers. *Charter School Laws: Do They Measure Up?* Washington, DC, 1996.

In this report, the union examines charter school laws and how they operate from state to state.

American Federation of Teachers. *Making Standards Matter, 1996: An Annual, Fifty-State Report on Efforts to Raise Academic Standards.* Washington, DC, 1996.

This report makes recommendations for standards of operation for charter schools that the union has identified as being of utmost importance. The report then examines charter schools state by state to apply the standards in the interest of evaluating the charter schools studied.

American Federation of Teachers. *National Education Standards and Assessment.* Washington, DC, 1992.

This report, an AFT convention resolution, speaks to educational standards and how they should apply to all public schools, including charter schools.

American Federation of Teachers. *Resolution on Charter Schools.* Anaheim, CA, July 1994.

This resolution, adopted by the AFT national convention, states the union's position on the charter school movement. It brings to the forefront questions that citizens need to be asking when evaluating the concept of charter schools.

American Federation of Teachers. **"U.S. Education: The Task before Us."** Washington, DC, 1992.

This report, an AFT convention resolution, addresses how schools must change and the formidable problems and issues that face school reform.

Shanker, A. **"Classrooms Held Hostage: Restoring Order in Our Schools."** Speech to the AFT Conference on Discipline and Safety. Washington, DC, 3 February 1995.

In this highly critical speech, Shanker speaks out against conditions in the classrooms and emphasizes how educational workers must begin to construct a curriculum that works for children.

Shanker, A. **"Making Standards Count: The Case for Student Incentives."** Speech to a Brookings Institute conference. Washington, DC, 18 May 1994.

Here, former AFT president Albert Shanker makes a plea for the types of standards we should be looking at when examining, evaluating, and analyzing both student and school achievement.

Shanker, A. Untitled speech to the National Press Club. Washington, DC, 31 March 1998.

In this speech, Shanker makes his claim for the charter school idea. He lays out his reasoning and in doing so, indicates significant movement in union embracement of the idea of charter schools.

Shanker, A. **"Where We Stand, Every School a Charter."** *New York Times,* 11 December 1994.

In this article, Shanker calls on every school to become a charter school and argues that the charter school idea should be the benchmark for all public schools.

Government Publications

With the huge growth and development of charter schools throughout the United States, government publications that evaluate and discuss aspects of charter school legislation have become more available. The following items represent just some of the publications that are available through federal and state governments.

Bierlein, L. *Charter Schools: Initial Findings.* Denver, CO: Education Commission of the States, March 1996.

This report publishes initial findings on charter schools and looks at the regulations that have been waived by many schools and how they might be doing as public entities by monitoring charter school legislation to identify nuances in the law, state-by-state.

Bierlein, L., and M. Fulton. *Emerging Issues in Charter School Financing.* Policy brief on charter school financing. Denver, CO: Education Commission of the States, May 1996.

In this report, the focus of the commentary is on funding and financing. The policy brief examines some of the problems charter schools face in the area of financing.

Blackorby, J., K. Finnegan, and L. Anderson. *Evaluation of Charter School Effectiveness.* Report prepared for the State of California Office of Legislative Analyst. Menlo Park, CA: SRI International, 1997.

This report, prepared for the state government, presents an evaluation of the work of charter schools within the state of California.

Budde, R. *Education by Charter: Restructuring Our Schools and School Districts.* Andover, MA: Regional Laboratory for Educational Improvement of the Northeast and Islands, 1989.

This report serves as a proponent of the charter school idea and posits it as a significant reform measure that promises to save public schools.

Clayton Foundation for the Colorado Department of Education. *1997 Colorado Charter School Evaluation Study.* Denver, CO, 1997.

This study is specific to Colorado and examines the laws, governance procedures, and workings of the charter school movement in Colorado.

Commonwealth of Massachusetts Department of Education. *The Massachusetts Charter School Initiative: Expanding the Possibilities of Education.* Boston, MA, 1998.

A state-specific report that looks at one of the most controversial states to have adopted charter school legislation. Every aspect is examined as it promotes or retards the charter school movement.

District of Columbia Board of Education. *Charter School Application: 1996.* Washington, DC, June 1996.

The District of Columbia Board of Education has published an examination of the charter application that deals with what is contained in these applications and how they are dealt with by government agencies.

Education Commission of the States. *Clearinghouse Issues Brief: Charter Schools.* Denver, CO, January 1996.

A general discussion of charter schools with a focus on what is working and what is not.

Education Commission of the States. *Clearinghouse Notes: Charter Schools.* Denver, CO, June 1994.

This report, the first of a series, attempts to examine the charter school movement as an educational reform movement.

Medler, A., and J. Nathan. *Charter Schools: What Are They up To?* Denver, CO: Education Commission of the States, August 1995.

A highly favorable view of charter schools, this report of a 1995 survey, compiled with the help of charter activist Joe Nathan, looks at what charter schools were doing at the time.

RPP International, University of Massachusetts. *A Study of Charter Schools: First Five-Year Report.* Washington, DC: U.S. Department of Education, 1997.

This first five-year report, issued by the University of Massachusetts, examines and analyzes what the charter movement has or has not accomplished.

Texas Board of Education. *Texas Open-Enrollment Charter Schools: Second Year Evaluation.* Austin, TX, 1997–1998.

This report looks specifically at the state of Texas, especially open-enrollment charter schools and how they are progressing in accordance with state educational standards.

U.S. Department of Education. *A Look at Charter Schools.* Washington, DC, March 1996.

The U.S. government examines charter schools as a reform movement in education. This work examines issues of race, class, admission policies, governance, and accountability.

U.S. Department of Education. *A Nation at Risk: Imperative for Education Reform.* Washington, DC: National Commission on Excellence in Education, 1983.

This famous report, produced during the Reagan years, sparked a new way of looking at schools and education and became a catalyst for educational reform controversies.

U.S. Department of Education. *A National Study of Charter Schools.* Washington, DC: Office of Educational Research and Improvement, 1998.

This national study of charter schools attempts to compare and contrast these schools throughout the United States.

U.S. Department of Education. *The State of Charter Schools 2000: Fourth Year Report.* Washington, DC, 2000.

This fourth report by the U.S. Department of Education is a continuation of previous examinations of the charter school movement and the political and financial problems that face charter schools.

U.S. Department of Education. *A Study of Charter Schools: Second Year Report.* Washington, DC, 1998.

This report by the Department of Education is essentially a report card on the charter school movement, and it points to problems and benefits.

U.S. General Accounting Office. *Charter Schools: New Models for Public Schools Provide Opportunities and Challenges.* Washington, DC, 1995.

Because they are proposed as new models for change, this report examines charter schools as an antidote to what the Accounting Office sees as problems with public schools.

Urahn, S., and D. Stewart. *Minnesota Charter Schools.* Minneapolis, MN: Minnesota House of Representatives Research Department, December 1994.

State-specific, this report looks at one of the first states to pass charter legislation. The report seeks to understand how charter schools have changed educational policies and procedures in Minnesota.

Private and Public Think Tank Publications

Becker, H., and K. Nakagawa. *Parent Involvement Contracts in California Charter Schools: Strategy for Education Improvement or Method of Exclusion?* Los Alamitos, CA: Southwest Regional Laboratory, April 1995.

This report advocates the participation of parents in charter school start-up and governance. It also looks at situations in which parents have been active in the charter school movement and the supposed consequences.

Berman, P., L. Diamond, and E. Premack. *Making Charter Schools Work.* Berkeley, CA: Institute for Policy Analysis and Research, June 1995.

Can charter schools work, and if so how? This report looks at the issues that fuel charter schools and what might be done to make the schools successful.

Bierlein, L., and L. Mulholland. *Charter School Update and Observations Regarding Initial Trends and Impacts.* Phoenix: Morrison Institute for Public Policy, April 1995.

Specifically looking at charter schools in Arizona, one of the most controversial states with charter school legislation, this report looks at the updates in practices and makes observations and evaluations.

Bierlein, L., and L. Mulholland. *Comparing Charter School Laws.* Phoenix: Morrison Institute for Public Policy, September 1994.

State by state, this report compares and contrasts state charter school laws.

Carnegie Forum on Education and the Economy. *A Nation Prepared: Teachers for the 21st Century.* Hyattsville, MD, 1986.

Looking at teaching and learning in the twenty-first century, this report speaks to what is necessary for effective teaching and educational reform as we enter the new millenium.

Chubb, J., and T. Moe. *Politics, Markets, and America's Schools.* Washington, DC: Brookings Institute, 1990.

A landmark book and one thought to spark the voucher movement in education. In this book, Moe and Chubb argue against public schools and why they feel they cannot and do not work.

Cobb, J., and G. Glass. **"Ethnic Segregation in Arizona Charter Schools."** *Education Policy Analysis Archives* 7, no. 1 (14 January 1999): 1–39.

This report looks at the issue of segregation in Arizona charter schools and why it exists.

Corwin, R., and M. Dianda. *Vision and Reality: A First Year Look at California's Charter Schools.* Los Alamitos, CA: Southwest Regional Laboratory, May 1994.

This work looks at the claims, visions, and actual practice of charter schools in California.

Corwin, R., and J. Flaherty, eds. *Freedom and Innovation in California Charter Schools.* Los Alamitos, CA: Southwest Regional Laboratory, November 1995.

In this report the emphasis is on the type of freedom and innovation the authors believe charter schools offer. They also offer recommendations to strengthen charter schools by providing more freedom from government regulation.

Finn, C., L. Bierlein, and B. Manno. *Charter Schools in Action: A First Look.* Washington, DC: Hudson Institute, January 1996.

A highly favorable look at charter schools in action. Chester Finn is a well-known advocate of privatized schooling and has embraced charter school movements as a beginning toward that end.

McDonnel, L., and A. Pascal. *Teacher Unions and Educational Reforms.* Santa Monica, CA: RAND, April 1988.

This work discusses what the authors believe is the need for changing roles between unions and the movement toward educational reform. The report calls for a different role of unions in education.

McGree, K. *Charter Schools: Early Findings.* Austin, TX: Southwest Educational Development Laboratory, 1995.

This report looks at charter school developments and compares and contrasts what was believed when they began and what is actually known now.

McGree, K. *Redefining Education Governance: The Charter School Concept.* Austin, TX: Southwest Educational Development Laboratory, 1995.

In this book, the author looks critically at current educational power and control and proposes that charter schools offer a means to redefine how schools are governed and run.

Millot, M. *Autonomy, Accountability, and the Values of Public Education: A Comparative Assessment of Charter School Statutes Leading to Model Legislation.* Santa Monica, CA: RAND, December 1994.

This report is centered on accountability in education and examines the assessment of schools through the glass of charter school legislation and reality.

Books and Journals

Ascher, C., N. Fruchter, and R. Berne. *Hard Lessons: Public Schools and Privatization.* New York: Twentieth-Century Fund Press, 1996.

What have we learned about privatization and public schools? This book looks at the issue in a way that helps the reader see why the movement for privatization is taking place.

Broderick, C. **"Rocky Mountain Rift: In the Mile-High City of Denver, a Maverick School Board Challenges the State's Charter School Law."** *American School Board Journal* 182, no. 10 (October 1995): 32–34.

What happens when a charter school law is challenged? That is the emphasis of this journal article, in which discussion is centered on the state Colorado.

Carnoy, M. **"Do Vouchers Improve Education?"** Paper presented at the Ford Foundation Constituency Building for School Reform Initiative, New York, 1998.

This paper criticizes the idea of vouchers and asks if the voucher movement will improve education. The author presents his reasoning as to why it will not.

Carnoy, M. **"School Improvement: Is Privatization the Answer?"** In *Decentralization and School Improvement: Can We Fulfill the Promise?* pp. 1–20. Ed. J. H. and M. Carnoy. San Francisco, CA: Jossey-Bass, 1993.

Is privatization of schools the answer to what is ailing public schools? This book examines this question and more in an attempt to forge a comprehensive approach to school reform.

"Charter School News." *Education Week,* 2 February 2000.

This article provides contemporary news about what some charter schools are doing.

Eberts, R., and A. Stone. ***Unions and Public Schools.*** Lexington, MA: Lexington Books, 1984.

What is the role of unions in public schools? Should they have a role? Does the role need to be redefined? This book takes up these issues.

Fine, M. ***Democratizing Choice: Reinventing Public Education.*** New York: City University of New York Graduate Center, 1993.

This famous author looks at urban schools and what they are doing with the charter concept. Her book gives readers the voices of teachers, administrators, parents, and students.

Hart, J. **"MCAS Scores of Charters Fail to Meet Expectations."** *Boston Globe,* 14 December 1998.

How many charter schools are actually functioning as planned? What about the ones that do not make it? This article looks at failing charter schools and discusses why they fail.

Kearney, C. P., and M. L. Arnold. **"Market Driven Schools and Educational Choices."** *Theory into Practice* 33, no. 1 (Spring 1994): 112–117.

Highly critical of market-driven schools, this article frames the issue in terms of choice and what that might mean for the nation's system of education.

Lopez, A., A. S. Wells, and J. J. Holme. **"Creating Charter School Communities: Identity Building, Diversity, and Selectivity."** Paper presented at the annual meeting of the American Educational Research Association, San Diego, 1998.

In this paper, the authors look at issues of discrimination and racial practices in charter school admissions. They also examine the notion of diversity and selectivity as social constructs.

Nathan, J. *Charter Schools: Creating Hope and Opportunity for American Education.* San Francisco: Jossey-Bass, 1996.

The best contemporary book favorable to the charter school idea, it discusses problems with public education and how charter schools can be constructed to overcome these perceived problems.

Nathan, J. **"Possibilities, Problems, and Progress: Early Lessons from the Charter School Movement."** *Phi Delta Kappan* 78, no. 1 (September 1996): 18–23.

The article praises charter schools but also points out problems. The author is highly supportive of the idea of charter school reform.

Rhim, L. M. **"Franchising Public Education: An Analysis of Charter Schools and Private Education Management Companies."** Paper presented at the American Education Research Association, San Diego, 1998.

This paper looks at educational maintenance organizations (EMOs). It specifically examines private management companies that make claims to run public schools with public funds.

Scherer, M. M. **"New Options for Public Education."** *Educational Leadership* 54, no. 2 (October 1996): 14–26.

In this article, charter schools are presented as a new option for what ails U.S. education.

Semple, M. **"Legal Issues in Charter Schooling."** *School Administrator* 52, no. 8 (August 1995): 24–26.

In this article, the administrator of a one school is asked to consider the legal issues involved in running a charter school.

Toch, T. **"Education Bazaar."** *U.S. News and World Report*, 27 April 1998.

Are we selling out our schools? What is this thing called educational reform? This article presents those issues clearly.

Tyack, D., and L. Cuban, L. *Tinkering towards Utopia: A Century of Public School Reform.* Cambridge, MA: Harvard University Press, 1995.

What have so-called educational reform efforts really accomplished? This book looks at educational reform movements, of which charter schools are just one form.

Vine, P. **"To Market, to Market: The School Business Sells Kids Short."** *Nation Magazine*, 8–15 September 1997.

This article makes the point that privatization is selling children short and ruining education. Highly controversial but compelling in its argumentation.

Wells, A. S., and R. L. Crain. *Stepping over the Color Line: African American Students in White Suburban Schools.* New Haven, CT: Yale University Press, 1997.

How are African Americans being served by the charter schools? What is their experience in public schools? This work examines the color issue in education.

Winerip, M. **"Schools for Sale."** *New York Times Magazine*, 4 June 1998.

Are we selling our schools to think tanks, private managerial firms, private curriculum companies, and the like? This article examines the privatization of all aspects of schools.

Yamashiro, K., and L. Carlos. *More on Charter Schools.* San Francisco: WestEd, 1996.

A thoughtful and comprehensive discussion of charter schools as a movement and as a reality.

Zollers, N., and A. Ramanathan. **"For Profit Charter Schools and Students with Disabilities."** *Phi Delta Kappan* (December 1998): 297.

What about students with disabilities? How are they faring in charter schools? This article examines the selection process for assuring equal access to charter schools for disabled persons.

NONPRINT RESOURCES

Nonprint resources for charter schools are best found on the internet. Although many educational organizations and their websites are mentioned in Chapter 7, the following include more links that offer on-line information about public education and charter schools.

American Association of School Administrators
http://www.aasa.org

This organization is devoted to educational issues faced by the administrators and managers of schools.

California Network of Educational Charters
http://www.canec.org

A network of charter schools and their advocates, this site has links to a multitude of parties interested in the charter movement.

Center on Reinventing Public Education
email: crpe@u.washington.edu

This center provide ideas on how schools might be reinvented to meet the needs of history. The site offers links and resources for people interested in the multitude of issues facing reform efforts in education.

Charter School Resource Center
http://www.pioneerinstitute.org

This center devotes itself to providing all and any resources needed to those wishing to start a charter school.

Corporate Watch
http://www.corpwatch.org

Corporate Watch provides news, analysis, research tools, and action resources to respond to corporate activity around the globe. The organization talks with people who are directly affected by corporate abuses as well as with others fighting for corporate accountability, human rights, and social and environmental justice. As part of the independent media, Corporate Watch is free of corporate sponsorship. The parent organization is the Transnational Resource and Action Center (TRAC), based in San Francisco. Corporate Watch seeks to monitor the influence of corporations in all areas of education.

Labor Notes
http://www.labornotes.org

Labor Notes is a nonprofit organization for union activists founded in 1979. It is devoted to discussing conditions for educational workers and what proposals for change might mean to them. The organization publishes the monthly magazine *Labor Notes,* which contains news of the labor movement.

National Coalition of Education Activists
email: members@aol.com/nceaweb

This coalition of activists attempts to unite people who are interested in realistic and progressive social change in education.

National Commission on Teaching and America's Future
http://www.tc.columbia.edu/`teachcomm

The National Commission on Teaching and America's Future treats every issue that confronts education today. The website gives links and resources along with opportunities to contact key players and members in the educational arena.

Network of Educators on the Americas
http://www.teachingforchange.org
e-mail: necadc@aol.com

The Network of Educators on the Americas is a think tank that provides a multitude of information on everything from charter schools to educational reform in integration.

Teachers Union Reform Network of AFT-NEA Locals
http://www.turnexchange.net
e-mail: urbanski@servtech.com

An alliance of two powerful teachers' unions, this network attempts to frame the issue of educational reform in ideas central to teachers, parents, and educational workers.

Trinational Coalition in Defense of Public Education: Canada, United States, and Mexico
e-mail: sanpatricio@igc.org

This organization is committed to the support and continuance of public education. It is a North American organization that addresses issues in the United States, Canada, and Mexico.

Appendix A

●❖ Comparison of State Standard Development and Charter School Requirements

States	Progress Toward Standards	Charter School Laws
Alaska	Adopted standards in English, math, and science; not specific enough to establish a core curriculum.	Charter schools do not have to meet state standards.
Arizona	Current drafts meet common core criteria, but are considered "borderline" and will need to be improved.	Charter schools must meet state standards.
Arkansas	None of the curriculum frameworks, except science, is detailed enough to meet the criteria.	Charter schools must meet state standards
California	Frameworks are not clear and detailed enough at the K–8 level and, thus, do not meet the criteria. New standards called Challenge standards are being developed.	Charter schools must meet state standards.
Colorado	Adopted standards meet AFT criteria.	Charter schools must meet state standards but are not required to take state assessments.
Connecticut	Guides are available in core subjects. Math and science are the only subjects that meet AFT criteria.	Charter schools do not have to meet state standards.
Delaware	Standards developed in core subjects. Meet AFT criteria.	Charter schools must meet state standards.

States	Progress Toward Standards	Charter School Laws
Florida	New frameworks meet common core criteria.	Charter schools do not have to meet state standards.
Georgia	Quality core curriculum in core subjects. Meet AFT criteria.	Charter schools must meet state standards.
Hawaii	Content and performance standards in core subjects. Two areas are borderline but meet the AFT criteria.	Charter schools must meet state standards.
Illinois	Process of revising academic standards is under way. Draft document is considered borderline, but meets AFT criteria.	Charter schools must meet state standards.
Kansas	Standards in core subjects emphasize skill over content. Do not meet AFT criteria.	Focus on outcome and and results. Do not have to meet state standards.
Louisiana	Curriculum guides in core subjects. English and social studies are under development; math and science do not meet AFT criteria.	Must meet minimum graduation requirements and required course study.
Massachusetts	Science framework exemplary, math is borderline, and English and social studies do not meet AFT criteria.	Charter schools must meet state standards.
Michigan	Draft standards in core subjects meet criteria but are considered borderline.	Charter schools must meet state standards.
Minnesota	Developing "basic requirements." But these are not specific enough to meet AFT criteria.	Charter schools must meet state standards.

States	Progress Toward Standards	Charter School Laws
New Hampshire	Curriculum frameworks in core subjects meet AFT criteria.	Charter schools do not have to meet state standards.
New Jersey	Draft standards in core subjects stress skills over content. Only science meets AFT criteria.	Charter schools must meet state standards.
New Mexico	Math and science meet criteria; English and social studies are under development.	Charter schools must meet state standards.
North Carolina	Standard course of study for each subject. Math strong, but other subjects do not meet AFT criteria.	Charter schools must meet state standards.
Rhode Island	English and math frameworks do not meet the criteria; science is borderline, and the state is not developing a social studies framework.	Charter schools must meet state standards.
South Carolina	Math and science standards meet criteria. English does not meet criteria, and there is no framework for social studies.	Charter schools must meet state standards.
Texas	Essential knowledge and skills in core subjects meet the AFT criteria.	Charter schools must meet state standards.
Wisconsin	Guides to curriculum planning in core subjects do not meet AFT criteria.	Not specified in the law.
Wyoming	No state standards in core subjects.	Not specified in the law.

Source: American Federation of Teachers. *Measuring Up: The AFT Criteria for Good Charter School Legislation.* AFT: Washington, DC, 1996.

Appendix B

●✦ State Testing Requirements

States	Uses the Same Test as Other Public Schools
Alaska	No
Arizona	Yes
Arkansas	No
California	Yes
Colorado	No, but the Department of Education can require that charter school students take the state assessments in order to make comparisons with state results.
Connecticut	Yes
Delaware	Yes
Florida	Yes
Georgia	No
Hawaii	Not specified
Illinois	Yes
Kansas	Yes
Louisiana	Yes
Massachusetts	Yes
Michigan	Yes
Minnesota	Not specified
New Hampshire	Yes
New Jersey	Yes
New Mexico	Not specified
North Carolina	Yes
Rhode Island	Yes
South Carolina	Yes
Texas	Yes
Wisconsin	Yes
Wyoming	Not specified

Source: American Federation of Teachers. *Measuring Up: The AFT Criteria for Good Charter School Legislation.* AFT: Washington, DC, 1996.

Appendix C

•◦ Admissions Policies

States	Admissions Policy
Alaska	Target age or grade level; target students who would benefit from teaching strategy or method
Arizona	Geographic preference
Arkansas	Same as public schools
California	Open to all students; conversion schools must give preference to students within attendance areas
Colorado	Open to all students
Connecticut	
Delaware	Some preferences given to conversion school siblings, at-risk pupils, and geographic location
Florida	Allows for sibling preference, attendance area preference, and at-risk student concentration
Georgia	Students in school district
Hawaii	Currently enrolled students
Illinois	Open to all children within the geographic boundaries
Kansas	Must reflect the racial and socioeconomic composition of the district
Louisiana	Must enroll same percentage of at-risk students as reside in district
Massachusetts	School can set admission standards based on academic ability

States	Admissions Policy
Michigan	Same criteria that districts are allowed to impose
Minnesota	Can target at-risk population
New Hampshire	May select students based on aptitude specified in the academic goals of the charter
New Jersey	Open to all students, but the charter school may establish reasonable criteria for admissions
New Mexico	
North Carolina	Open to any student who is qualified for admission to a public school
Rhode Island	May establish reasonable criteria to evaluate prospective students; preference to students who are enrolled in the district
South Carolina	Open to any student who is qualified for admission to a public school
Texas (applies to open-enrollment and campus charters)	Open to all students; may exclude students with documented history of criminal offenses, court adjudication, or discipline problems
Wisconsin	Students in enrollment area
Wyoming	Preference to students in enrollment area

Source: American Federation of Teachers. *Measuring Up: The AFT Criteria for Good Charter School Legislation.* AFT: Washington, DC, 1996.

Appendix D

●◆ Teacher Professionalism

States	Collective Bargaining	Certification Requirements
Alaska	Yes, unless excluded by the local district and bargaining agent	Yes
Arizona	No	No. Each charter school establishes qualifications
Arkansas	No	Yes
California	Teachers can opt to remain in the unit, organize separately, or not at all	No
Colorado	Yes, if public school conversion	No
Connecticut	Yes. Agreement may be modified consistent with charter	Up to 50 percent of the teachers may be uncertified
Delaware	Employees have the right to organize; may not be part of the existing unit	Up to 35 percent of the teachers may be uncertified; alternative certification specified in the law
Florida	Employees have the right to organize; may not be part of the existing unit	No; each charter school establishes qualifications
Georgia	*	*
Hawaii	Yes	*
Illinois	Separate and distinct from the local bargaining unit	No qualifications specified in the law

States	Collective Bargaining	Certification Requirements
Kansas	If granted by local district covered by bargaining agent	*
Louisiana	Covered by the collective bargaining agreement unless specified otherwise in the charter	25 percent of the teachers may be uncertified
Massachusetts	Yes, but in separate bargaining units	No
Michigan	Only if the charter is granted by the district; when charter granted by state colleges, universities, or county district then not specified	Yes, unless college professor at state college or university is sponsoring the charter school
Minnesota	Yes, but not part of any other bargaining unit unless agreed to by all parties	Yes
New Hampshire	Right to bargain as separate unit; teacher must withdraw from other bargaining unit	50 percent of the teachers at a charter school must be certified or have three years of teaching experience
New Jersey	Yes, if it is a conversion school; if a new school, only with the agreement of the parties	Yes
New Mexico	*	*
North Carolina	No	Allows for 25 percent of elementary and 50 percent of secondary charter school teachers to be uncertified
Rhode Island	Yes	Yes

States	Collective Bargaining	Certification Requirements
South Carolina	No	25 percent of staff uncertified; if a public school conversion, 10 percent may be uncertified
Texas	Texas has no collective bargaining law for public employees but has the right to confer	No
Wisconsin	Yes	No
Wyoming	No	No

*The law is silent; but all charter schools are converted public schools, and the rules and regulations governing other public schoolteachers apply to charter schoolteachers as well.

Source: American Federation of Teachers. *Measuring Up: The AFT Criteria for Good Charter School Legislation.* AFT: Washington, DC, 1996.

✎ Index

About the Author

Danny Weil was a public interest attorney who stopped practicing law to become a bilingual kindergarten teacher. He has taught primary school, junior high school, high school, and college. He is the author of many books on critical thinking and critical pedagogy and is a consultant for school districts throughout the United States, Mexico, and Puerto Rico. He holds a Ph.D. in both education and law.